Karate Sports Academy

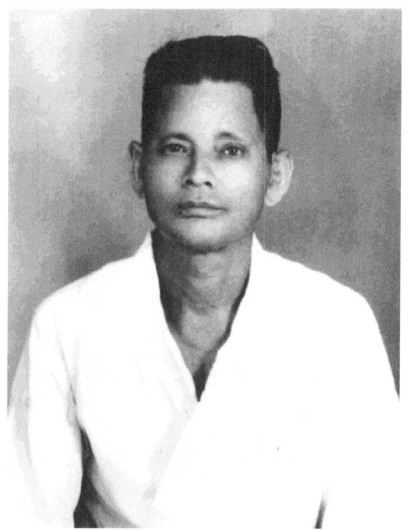

Tatsuo Shimabuku

Student Handbook

2

TABLE OF CONTENTS

NON-TRADITIONAL KATAS

HISTORY

MARTIAL ARTS TOPIC SUMMARIES

PERSONAL NOTES

6

GENERAL SCHOOL INFORMATION

About the school

Name
> Karate Sports Academy

Teacher
> Scott Britt
> isshin-ryu@hotmail.com
> 423-539-3687

Website
> www.petemillskarate.com

Facebook
> "Scott Britt", Isshinryu of Oak Ridge group

Mission statement:
> Our mission is to teach karate in a Christ-like manner in such a way to make it practical and applicable for self-defense while avoiding risk of injury.

Extended mission statement:
> Our goal is teach traditional Isshinryu karate to make it applicable for self-defense to all ages and abilities. This will be done by a staged approach to Kata, progressing to more and more realistic training in Bunkai. Pads and heavy bags will be used to simulate full contact to avoid risk of injury, while all sparring/bunkai drills will be light contact for the lower ranks and medium contact for upper ranks. Basic skills in Ju-jitsu, weapons defense, and tournament play will be taught as well. Every class will end in prayer, and every effort will be made to teach Karate in a Christ-like manner and from a biblical perspective.

Introduction

This book is designed to have all relevant information needed for the student of Isshinryu karate through the first several belts, as well as a general resource for history and topics relating to karate. I have found over the years that the world of Karate is fascinating, with always more to learn no matter how long you are in it. I look forward to working with you in exploring this world, and bettering skills that may one day keep you safe from danger.

It is a given that, like learning any other skill such as piano, the limited class time each week is not sufficient to become great. This means that practice at home is a requirement, and this book is meant to serve as a reference for that practice. Keep in mind, it is difficult to learn from scratch a complex movement from a photo in a book – therefore, the portions with step-by-step photographs are meant to serve as memory-joggers for what has already been learned in class.

Notes on the 2nd Edition

The second edition is over double the length of the first edition. While a good portion comes from an addition of reference content (photos of the first few katas, expanded history section, etc.), there are some significant changes to the ranking outline. Allow me to explain what they are, and why they were made.

There are two main changes, both resulting from my years of teaching observation; the first observation was that while katas were being learned, the bunkai within them was not being practiced to the point of proficiency to where it could actually be used to for defense in a high-stress situation. This was due to there being so many katas per belt to learn, there was not time to stop and focus on the bunkai before moving on to the next kata. So the first change is picking three kata to be core katas (Seisan, Naihanchi, and Wansu), and focusing on them through the first several belts, and the addition of Bunkai drills to the requirements. The other katas are learned latter, and without the focus on committing the bunkai to muscle memory (at this point). Keep in mind that by black belt, all the same katas are learned as before, just in a different order and with different emphasis. After first degree black belt more stress can be placed on the other kata's bunkai.

The second change is the addition of an "extra credit," requirement to each belt, which can now include a slew of non-traditional katas. This change came from the fact that many new students are excited to start learning weapons, grappling, etc., but are disappointed when those subjects do not come until much later in their training. Now a student can pick what most interests them (always a good approach to learning), such as the Bo staff, and learn a 12-step mini-kata that works the fundamentals of that weapon. These mini-katas were created by black belts within the school to learn the basics of each weapon (how to hold, basic strikes and blocks) in a format that could be learned in one class.

Therefore, I have both expanded and contracted the requirements; I have added a wide range of electives for variety, and narrowed the focus of the traditional katas to perfect a few rather than having surface knowledge of many. My hope is that this will keep your martial arts training both engaging and practical.

Thank you!

Scott

P.S. – My thanks to those who helped me with the photos and katas for this book; Jeff Poore, Orsolya Karácsony, Reagan and Renae Dishman, Brian Summers, and Parker Richardson.

Rules of the Dojo

1. Treat your belt with respect
2. Never wear a karate belt outside the dojo
3. Remove shoes when stepping onto the mat
4. Turn away from instructors when adjusting gi/belt
5. Bow when handing/receiving a weapon
6. Fighting outside the dojo (not in self-defense) is strictly forbidden! This is grounds for instant dismissal
7. Bow when starting and ending a sparring match
8. Gi's should be clean and presentable
9. Keep fingernails and toenails trimmed
10. Before class, stretch or run kata
11. No jewelry may be worn during class (exception – wedding rings)
12. If your are unable to come to class, be sure to let an instructor know
13. If you have a cold or are contagious, please stay home
14. Do not interrupt class – raise your hand
15. No roughhousing/ horseplay
16. Cup and mouthpiece are requirements for sparring

Terminology

Commonly used words are in **Bold.**

Word	Pronunciation	Meaning
Karate		Empty hand
Isshinryu	[ish-in-rue]	One heart way
Megami	[ma-ga-mee]	Isshinryu patch
Kata		Forms
Karate Ka		Student of karate
Sensei	[sin-say]	Teacher (1st – 5th Dan)
Shehan	[she-hon]	Master (6th – 8th Dan)
Grandmaster		9th – 10th Dan
Dojo		Karate school
Gi	[gee]	Uniform
Obi	[obee]	Belt
Dan rank		Black belt rank
Kyu rank	[Q rank]	White – Brown belt
Rei	[ray]	Formal bow
Hajame	[Ha-gee-may]	Begin (sparring)
Yame	[ya-may]	Stop (sparring)
Kiai	[kee-yi]	Yell
Kumite	[koo-mit-ay]	Sparring
Bunkai	[bunk-eye]	Application (of kata movements)
Nukite	[nu-kit-ay]	Gouge
Hai	[hi]	Yes
Waza		Technique
Tatsuo Shimabuku	[tot-sue-o shim-a-boo-koo]	Founder of Isshinryu

Counting			
One	Ichi	Six	Roko
Two	Ni	Seven	Shichi
Three	San	Eight	Hachi
Four	Shi	Nine	Ku
Five	Go	Ten	Ju

14

15

YELLOW BELT MATERIAL

Student Creed

1. **I will develop myself in a positive manner and avoid anything that would reduce my mental growth or my physical health.**

2. **I will develop self-discipline in order to bring out the best in myself and others.**

3. **I will use what I learn in class constructively and defensively: to help myself and my fellow man and never to be abusive or offensive.**

Chart 1

------- Single Strikes

1. **RFA/RH Straight Punch**
2. **RFA/RH Uppercut**
3. **LFA/LH Straight Punch**
4. **LFA/LH Uppercut**

------- Block/Strike combinations

5. **RFB/LH Leg Block – RH Straight Punch**
6. **RFB/LH Side Block – RH Straight Punch**
7. **RFB/LH Open Side Block – RH Gouge**
8. **RFB/LH Open Arc Sweep – RH Uppercut**
9. **RFB/LH Head Block – RH Straight Punch**
10. **RFB/LH Bridge of Nose – RH Straight Punch**

------- 3 sets of 2 (5 punches, weird set, T-stances)

11. **LFA/LH Leg Block – 5 Straight Punches**
12. **LFA/LH Side Block – 5 Straight Punches**

13. **LFA/LH Chop Midsection – RH Chop to Neck**
14. **LFA/RH Strike to Base of Ribs – LH same**

15. **RFB/LF T-Stance – R Elbow Strike**
15.b **RFB/LF T-Stance – LH open ark sweep, right upward elbow**

L = Left	H = Hand	B = Back
R = Right	F = Foot	A = Advance (Forward)

Note: After #4, repeating the move on the opposite side is assumed

Chart 2

1.   **Bend over touch floor**
2.   **Back bend - exhale 5 times**
3.   **Grab Heel w/opposite hand, push out**
4.   **Leg Stretches**

5.   **Straight Kick**
6.   **Cross Kick**
7.   **Forward on Angle Kick**
8.   **Side Kick – Heel and Edge of Foot**
9.   **Side Kick – Ball of Foot**
10. **Squat to Side and roundhouse Kick**
11. **Heel Push Kick**
12. **Knee strike**

13. **Push-Ups on Knuckles**
14. **Side Twist – Right & Left**
15. **Breathing – Up Inhale, Down Exhale**

Memory Aid: Kicks 5-8 are from inside to outside, kicks 9-12 are from outside to inside

Charts 1 with photos

1., 2. Punch | **3., 4.** Uppercut | **5.** Leg block, punch

6. Side block, punch | **7.** Open side block, gouge

8. Open arc sweep, uppercut | **9.** Head block, punch

10. Bridge of nose, punch | **11.** Leg block…

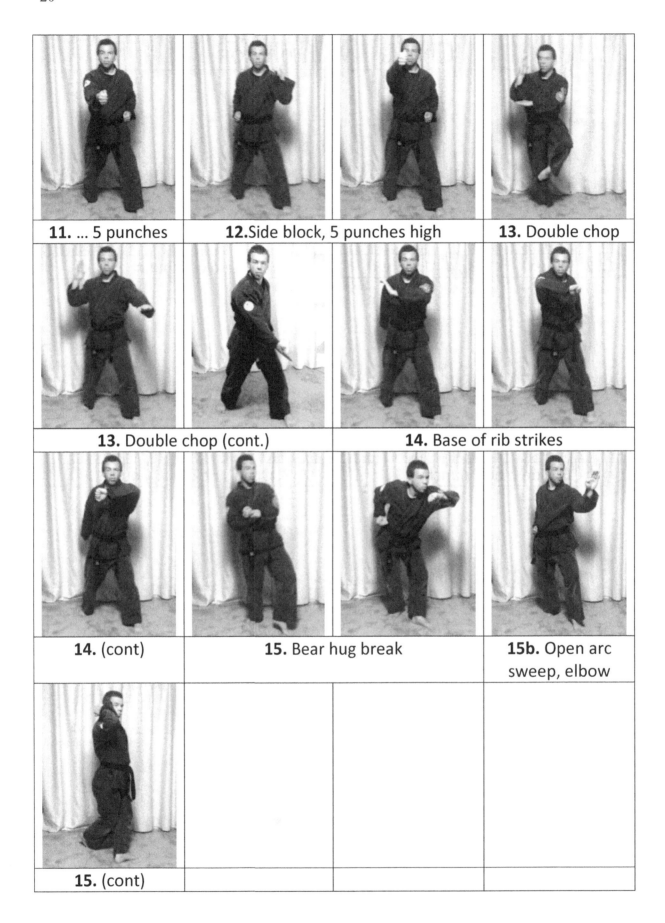

11. ... 5 punches	**12.** Side block, 5 punches high	**13.** Double chop

13. Double chop (cont.)   **14.** Base of rib strikes

14. (cont)	**15.** Bear hug break	**15b.** Open arc sweep, elbow

15. (cont)

Chart 2 with photos

1. Touch toes	**2.** Bend back	**3.** Leg ext.	**4.** Splits
5. Straight kick	**6.** Cross kick	**7.** Angle kick	**8.** Side kick
9. Turning snap kick		**10.** Roundhouse kick	
10. (Cont)	**11.** Heel push kick		**12.** Knee strike

12. (cont.)	13. Pushups	14. Side twists
15. Breathing		

How to Tie a Belt

Credit: http://www.kataaro.com/BeltTying.aspx

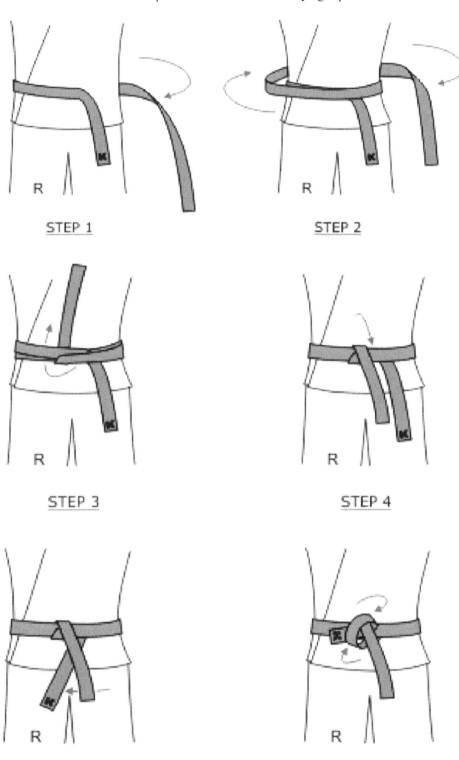

STEP 1

STEP 2

STEP 3

STEP 4

STEP 5

STEP 6

RANK REQUIREMENTS

Rank Advancement Outline

All rank except for yellow requires a minimum of three months attendance, no exceptions. There are no time requirements to go from white to yellow belt. Additional class credit may be earned though extracurricular activity (tournament attendance, homework assignments, etc. as determined by instructor). There are black stripes between belts, one for each requirement. After earning all stripes the student may test for the next belt, assuming the three-month time requirement is met. Students are allowed 2 mistakes per test. Tests will spot-check material from previous belt tests.

NOTE: EACH TEST HAS HISTORY QUESTIONS (see testing forms)

Yellow/White Belt
- Chart II
- Student Creed

Yellow Belt
- Chart I

Gold Belt
- Seisan
- Extra Credit

Orange Belt
- Naihanchi
- Seisan Bunkai
- Extra Credit

Green Belt
- Wansu
- Naihanchin Bunkai
- Extra Credit

Blue Belt
- Kata from Black Belt List

- Wansu Bunkai
- Extra Credit

Purple Belt
- Weapon kata
- Sanchin
- Extra Credit

Brown Belt
- Seiuchin
- First aid certification

Black Belt
- Sunsu
- Chinto
- Kusanku
- Kumite Rock
- Weapon Kata
- Extra Credit

Extra credit can consist of: (discuss with instructor beforehand)
- 1-2 page report
- Teaching a class
- Competing in a tournament
- Attending a seminar
- Demonstration of a non-traditional kata
- Learn kata(e.g., Kumite Rock) or First Aid early

Yellow/White Belt Test

Student Name _____ Reviewer Name _____ Score_____

Student Creed:

☐   1.   I will develop myself in a positive manner and avoid anything that would reduce my mental growth or my physical health.

☐   2.   I will develop self-discipline in order to bring out the best in myself and others.

☐   3.   I will use what I learn in class constructively and defensively: to help myself and my fellow man and never to be abusive or offensive.

Chart II:

☐   1.   BEND OVER TOUCH FLOOR.
☐   2.   BACK BEND – EXHALE 5 TIMES.
☐   3.   LH Grab Right Heel – RH Push Knee Down.
☐   4.   Leg Stretches.
☐   5.   Straight Kick.
☐   6.   Cross Kick.
☐   7.   Forward on Angle Kick.
☐   8.   Side Kick – Heel and Edge of Foot.
☐   9.   Side Kick – Ball of Foot.
☐   10.   Squat to Side and roundhouse Kick.
☐   11.   Heel Push Kick.
☐   12.   Knee strike.
☐   13.   Push-Ups on Knuckles.
☐   14.   Side Twist – Right & Left.
☐   15.   Breathing – Up Inhale – Down Exhale (10 Times).

History:

☐   The style of karate we study is called Isshinryu
☐   Isshinryu means "One Heart Way"
☐   The head over this dojo is Pete Mills
☐   Isshinryu is from Okinawa

Notes:

_____

_____

_____

Yellow Belt Test

Student Name _____ Reviewer Name _____ Score_____

Review:
- ☐ Student Creed
- ☐ Chart II

Chart I:
- ☐ 1. Straight Punch.
- ☐ 2. Uppercut.
- ☐ 5. Leg Block – Straight Punch.
- ☐ 6. Side Block – Straight Punch.
- ☐ 7. Open Side Block – Forward (Nukite) Gouge.
- ☐ 8. Open Arc Sweep – Uppercut.
- ☐ 9. Head Block – Straight Punch.
- ☐ 10. Bridge of Nose – Straight Punch.
- ☐ 11. Leg Block – 5 Straight Punches.
- ☐ 12. Side Block – 5 Straight Punches.
- ☐ 13. Chop to Midsection – Chop to Base of Neck.
- ☐ 14. Strike to Base of Ribs – Strike to Base of Ribs.
- ☐ 15.1 T Position – Elbow Strike.
- ☐ 15.2 Cat stance – upward Elbow Strike

History:
- ☐ Isshinryu was founded by <u>Tatsuo Shimabuku</u>
- ☐ Tatsuo Shimabuku was born in the village of <u>Chun</u> in <u>1908</u>
- ☐ Karate means <u>"empty hand"</u>
- ☐ Seisan means "<u>13</u>"

Notes:

_____
_____
_____
_____
_____
_____

Yellow/Orange (Gold) Belt Test

Student Name _____ Reviewer Name _____ Score_____

Review:
- ☐ Student Creed
- ☐ Chart I
- ☐ Chart II

Seisan:
- ☐ Ran kata without help

  _____

- ☐ Looked before turning

  _____

- ☐ Kept hand at hips when required

  _____

- ☐ Remembered to Kiai

  _____

- ☐ Feet in good, distinct, stance

  _____

Extra Credit:
- ☐ Completed, describe below

  _____

History:
- ☐ 1 Fact from Seisan history page
- ☐ Isshinryu has katas from Shorinryu, Gojuryu, and Kobudo
- ☐ Seiuchin is one of two Gojuryu katas (the other being Sanchin)
- ☐ Naihanchin was designed for hallways and against a wall

Notes:

_____
_____
_____
_____
_____
_____

Orange Belt Test

Student Name _____ Reviewer Name _____ Score_____

Review:
- ☐ Student Creed
- ☐ Chart I
- ☐ Chart II
- ☐ Seisan

Seisan Bunkai:
- ☐ Run kata, describing each moves Bunkai
  _____
- ☐ Perform Seisan Flow Drill I against non-compliant opponent
  _____
- ☐ Perform Seisan Flow Drill II against non-compliant opponent
  _____

Naihanchin:
- ☐ Ran kata without help
  _____
- ☐ Looked before turning
  _____
- ☐ Kept hand at hips when required
  _____
- ☐ Remembered to Kiai
  _____
- ☐ Feet in good, distinct, stance
  _____

Extra Credit:
- ☐ Completed, describe below
  _____

History:
- ☐ Tatsuo means "Dragon Man", and was not his given name
- ☐ Tatsuo Shimabuku died on May 30th, 1975
- ☐ 1 Fact from the Naihanchin history page
- ☐ Tatsuo taught: Harold Long, Don Nagle, Harold Mitchum, Steve Armstrong.

Notes: _____
_____
_____

Green Belt Test

Student Name _____ Reviewer Name _____ Score_____

Review:
- ☐ Student Creed
- ☐ Chart II
- ☐ Naihanchin
- ☐ Chart I
- ☐ Seisan / Bunkai

Naihanchin Bunkai:
- ☐ Run kata, describing each moves Bunkai

_____

- ☐ Perform Naihanchin Flow Drill I against non-compliant opponent

_____

- ☐ Perform Naihanchin Flow Drill II against non-compliant opponent

_____

Wansu:
- ☐ Ran kata without help

_____

- ☐ Looked before turning

_____

- ☐ Kept hand at hips when required

_____

- ☐ Remembered to Kiai

_____

- ☐ Feet in good, distinct, stance

_____

Extra Credit:
- ☐ Completed, describe below

_____

History:
- ☐ Isshinryu became a style on January 15th, 1956
- ☐ 1 Fact from the Wansu history page
- ☐ Wansu means "Hidden Fist"
- ☐ Tatsuo's teachers were Chotoku Kyan, Chojun Miyagi, and Choki Motobu

Notes:

_____
_____
_____

Blue Belt Test

Student Name _____ Reviewer Name _____ Score_____

Review:
- ☐ Student Creed
- ☐ Chart I
- ☐ Chart II
- ☐ Seisan / Bunkai
- ☐ Naihan. / Bunkai
- ☐ Wansu

Wansu Bunkai:
- ☐ Run kata, describing each moves Bunkai

  _____

- ☐ Perform Wansu Flow Drill I against non-compliant opponent

  _____

- ☐ Perform Wansu Flow Drill II against non-compliant opponent

  _____

Kata from Black belt list:
- ☐ Ran kata without help

  _____

- ☐ Looked before turning

  _____

- ☐ Kept hand at hips when required

  _____

- ☐ Remembered to Kiai

  _____

- ☐ Feet in good, distinct, stance

  _____

Extra Credit:
- ☐ Completed, describe: _____

History:
- ☐ Brief explanation of the isshinryu patch
- ☐ Chinto refers to the Chinese Sailor named Chinto
- ☐ Sanchin mean "Three Battles"
- ☐ Tatsuo taught: Harold Long, Don Nagle, Harold Mitchum, and Steve Armstrong.

Notes:

_____

_____

_____

Purple Belt Test

Student Name _____ Reviewer Name _____ Score_____

Review:
- ☐ Student Creed
- ☐ Chart I & II
- ☐ Black belt list kata
- ☐ Seisan / Bunkai
- ☐ Naihanchin / Bunkai
- ☐ Wansu / Bunkai

Sanchin Kata:
- ☐ Ran kata without help

  _____

- ☐ Maintained proper focus / tension throughout

  _____

- ☐ Feet in good, distinct, stance

  _____

Weapon Kata:
- ☐ Ran kata without help

  _____

- ☐ Looked before turning

  _____

- ☐ Kept hand at hips when required

  _____

- ☐ Remembered to Kiai

  _____

- ☐ Feet in good, distinct, stance

  _____

Extra Credit:
- ☐ Completed, describe below

  _____

History:
- ☐ Suensu is the only kata in isshinryu designed by Tatsuo.
- ☐ Kusank is a night kata
- ☐ Tatsuo's nephew, Angi Ueza, heads Isshinryu in Okinama
- ☐ Additional fact of your choosing

Notes:

_____

_____

_____

Brown Belt Test

Student Name _____ Reviewer Name _____ Score_____

Review:
☐ Student Creed   ☐ Naihanchin / Bunkai
☐ Chart I & II   ☐ Wansu / Bunkai
☐ Black belt list kata   ☐ Sanchin
☐ Seisan / Bunkai   ☐ Weapon Kata

First Aid Test:
☐ Describe Basics of First Aid (3 C's, CAB, etc)

_____

☐ Demonstrate First Aid for basic scenarios of testers choosing

_____

Seiunchin Kata:
☐ Ran kata without help

_____

☐ Looked before turning

_____

☐ Kept hand at hips when required

_____

☐ Remembered to Kiai

_____

☐ Feet in good, distinct, stance

_____

History:
☐ Kusaku was designed by <u>Chinese envoy</u> Kushanku
☐ Sunsu means <u>"Strong Man"</u>
☐ Learn Isshinryu Code
☐ Additional Fact of your choosing

Notes:

_____
_____
_____

1ˢᵗ Dan Black Belt Test

Student Name _____ Reviewer Name _____ Score_____

Review:
☐ Student Creed   ☐ Wansu / Bunkai
☐ Chart I & II   ☐ Sanchin
☐ Black belt list kata   ☐ Weapon Kata
☐ Seisan / Bunkai   ☐ Seiunchin
☐ Naihanchin / Bunkai   ☐ First Aid

Test will include the material above, as well as the material below (those that were not covered previously; one or more should have been covered under previous tests):

Black Belt
- Sunsu
- Chinto
- Kusanku
- Kumite Rock
- Weapon Kata
- Extra Credit

As you approach your black belt, a complete testing sheet will be provided you well in advance of the test. Test will be completed by a board of black belts, both from within this school and from partner dojos.

TRADITIONAL KATAS

Kiais in Kata

1) Seisan

    a) On first step-across kick

    b) On last kick

2) Seiuchin

    a) At fist hammer fist into left hand

    b) On last back fist, before open arc sweep

3) Naihanchin

    a) At last double punch, right before bowing out

4) Wansu

    a) On restrained punch right before start of wansu dump

    b) Eye rake at end of kata

5) Chinto

    a) On first double kick

    b) On kneeling punch at end of kata

6) Kusanku

    a) On first kneeling forearm strike

    b) On double kick at end of kata

7) Sunsu

    a) Third set of elbow strikes

    b) On first kick-side block-leg block combo at end of kata

8) Kusanku-sai

    a) Same place as Kusanku

9) Tokumine-no-kun

    a) On third thrust at beginning of kata

    b) Overhead swinging strike

10) Urashi No Kan bo

    a) On first thrust to fallen opponent

    b) Next to last stick

11) Chatan yara No sai

    a) First set of double punches

    b) On overhand strike at end of kata

12) Shishi-no-kun

    a) Stick in first series

    b) On first thrust to fallen opponent

Kata Footwork

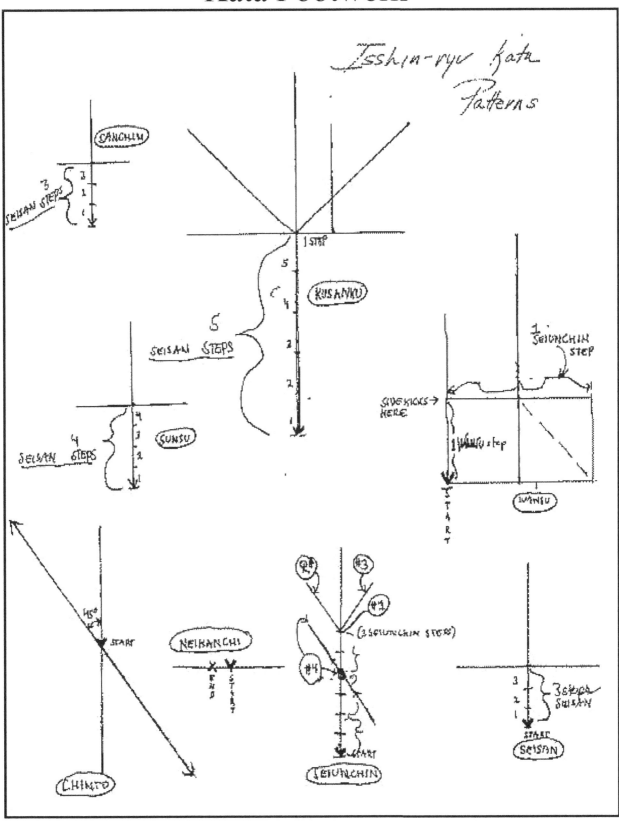

Basic stances

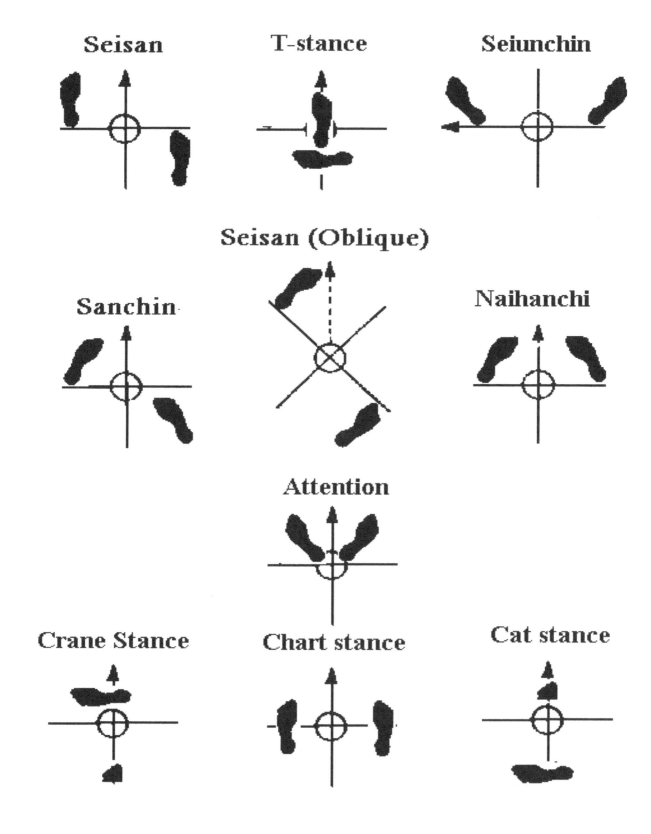

Seisan Kata

The photos of each movement are taken from the best angle, and not necessarily from the direction faced at the beginning of the kata. To tell which direction is being faced in the kata, refer to the arrow next to the movement number. See diagram below for an illustration looking down from above:

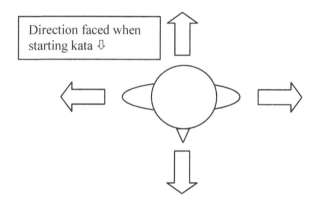

Direction faced when starting kata ⇩

Seisan

1. ⇩ Stand at attention	**2.** ⇩ Bow	**3.** ⇩ Salutation	**4.** ⇩ Ready stance
5. ⇩ Step up left foot, prepare for…	**6.** ⇩ Left side block	**7.** ⇩ Right hand punch	**8.** ⇩ Step up with right foot, left hand punch
9. ⇩ Step up with left foot, right hand punch	**10.** ⇩ Double-fist into center	**11.** ⇩ Half-step forward, double head-blocks	**12.** ⇧ X-block with 180° pivot

Seisan

13. ⇧ Double knife-hand downward strike	**14.** ⇧ Step forward w/ right foot, right inverted ridgehand	**15.** ⇧ Turn right hand over	**16.** ⇧ Pull elbow toward hip
17. ⇧ Step forward w/ left foot, left inverted ridgehand	**18.** ⇧ Turn left hand over	**19.** ⇧ Pull elbow toward hip	**20.** ⇧ Step forward w/ right foot, right inverted ridgehand
21. ⇧ Turn right hand over	**22.** ⇧ Pull right elbow down toward hip	**23.** ⇧ Stack hands on right hip	**24.** ⇐ Turn left, left hand side block

Seisan

25. ⇐ Right hand punch	**26.** ⇐ Left hand punch	**27.** ⇐ Right foot straight kick	**28.** ⇐ Right hand punch
29. ⇑ Stack hands on left hip	**30.** ⇒ Turn 180° (Seisan stance) right side block	**31.** ⇒ Left hand punch	**32.** ⇒ Right hand punch
33. ⇒ Left foot straight kick	**34.** ⇒ Left hand punch	**35.** ⇒ Stack hands on right hip, look left	**36.** ⇑ Turn left, left hand side block

Seisan

37. ⇧ Right hand punch	**38.** ⇧ Left hand punch	**39.** ⇧ Right foot straight kick	**40.** ⇧ Right hand punch
41. ⇧ Pivot right foot into Seiunchin stance	**42.** ⇧ Squat block	**43.** ⇩ Turn 180° and draw back	**44.** ⇩ Step out, right hand bridge-of-nose strike
45. ⇩ Draw back, drop right elbow	**46.** ⇩ Step across with left foot	**47.** ⇩ Right foot straight kick	**48.** ⇩ Straighten into Seisan stance, right leg block

46

Seisan

49. ⇩ Left hand punch	**50.** ⇩ Pivot left foot into Seiunchin stance, squat block	**51.** ⇧ Turn 180° and draw back	**52.** ⇧ Step out, left hand bridge-of-nose strike
53. ⇧ Draw back, drop left elbow	**54.** ⇧ Step across with right foot	**55.** ⇧ Left foot straight kick	**56.** ⇧ Straighten into Seisan stance, left hand leg block
57. ⇧ Right hand punch	**58.** ⇧ Pivot right foot into Seiunchin stance, squat block	**59.** ⇩ Turn 180° and draw back	**60.** ⇩ Step out, right hand bridge-of-nose strike

Seisan

61. ⇩ Straighten into Seisan stance, right leg block	**62.** ⇩ Left hand punch	**63.** ⇩ Pivot left foot into Seiunchin stance, squat block	**64.** ⇩ Draw back into cat stance, left open arc sweep
65. ⇩ Straighten into Seisan stance	**66.** ⇩ Right foot straight kick	**67.** ⇩ Right hand punch	**68.** ⇩ Extend left hand to meet right hand
69. ⇩ Draw back into cat stance	**70.** ⇩ Bring arms in circle to hips	**71.** ⇩ Right hand high, left hand low	**72.** ⇩ Bring feet together…

Seisan			
73. ⇩ Closing salutation	**74.** ⇩ Bow	**75.** ⇩ End of kata	

Naihanchi Kata

The photos of each movement are taken from the best angle, and not necessarily from the direction faced at the beginning of the kata. To tell which direction is being faced in the kata, refer to the arrow next to the movement number. See diagram below for an illustration looking down from above:

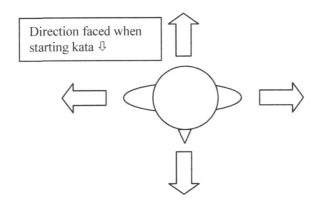

Direction faced when starting kata ⇩

Naihanchi

1. ⇩ Stand at attention	**2.** ⇩ Bow	**3.** ⇩ Salutation	**4.** ⇩ Turn feet into Naihanchi stance
5. ⇩ Cross right foot over left	**6.** ⇨ Step out with left foot, inverted ridgehand	**7.** ⇨ Right arm elbow strike into left hand	**8.** ⇩ Stack hands on left hip
9. ⇩ Draw up right foot	**10.** ⇦ Right hand leg block to right side	**11.** ⇦ Gouge right with left hand	**12.** ⇦ Step across with left foot

Naihanchi

13. ⇐ Draw up right foot	**14.** ⇓ Left hand inverted ridgehand	**15.** ⇓ Left hand hammer strike	**16.** ⇓ Right hand upward elbow strike
17. ⇓ Right hand backfist	**18.** ⇐ Draw up right foot	**19.** ⇐ Right hand backfist to right	**20.** ⇒ Draw up left foot
21. ⇒ Right hand hammerfist to left	**22.** ⇐ Stack hands on left hip, right foot up	**23.** ⇐ Both hands on hips preparing for...	**24.** ⇐ Double punch to the right

Naihanchi

25. ⇐ Right hand inverted rigehand to right	**26.** ⇐ Left elbow strike into right hand	**27.** ⇓ Stack hands on right hip	**28.** ⇒ Draw up left foot
29. ⇒ Left hand leg block to left	**30.** ⇒ Right hand gouge across to left, left hand stack	**31.** ⇒ Step across with right foot	**32.** ⇒ Draw left foot up
33. ⇓ Right hand inverted ridgehand to front	**34.** ⇓ Right hand downward hammerfist	**35.** ⇓ Left upwards elbow strike	**36.** ⇓ Left outward backfist

Naihanchi

37. ⇨ Draw up left foot	**38.** ⇨ Left hand backfist to left	**39.** ⇦ Draw up right foot	**40.** ⇦ Left hand hammer fist to right
41. ⇨ Stack hands on right hip, draw up left foot	**42.** ⇨ Both hands on hips preparing for...	**43.** ⇨ Double punch to left	**44.** ⇩ Draw feet together to stand at attention
45. ⇩ Closing salutation	**46.** ⇩ Bow	**47.** ⇩ End of kata	

Wansu Kata

The photos of each movement are taken from the best angle, and not necessarily from the direction faced at the beginning of the kata. To tell which direction is being faced in the kata, refer to the arrow next to the movement number. See diagram below for an illustration looking down from above:

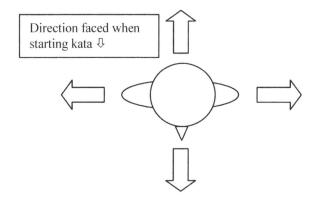

Wansu

1. ⇩ Stand at attention	**2.** ⇩ Bow	**3.** ⇩ Salutation	**4.** ⇩ Step out with right foot, left hand over right fist
5. ⇨ Left hand leg block to left	**6.** ⇨ Right hand punch to left	**7.** ⇩ Step up with left foot, left hand leg block	**8.** ⇩ Right hand punch
9. ⇩ Step up right foot, right hand open arc sweep	**10.** ⇩ Gouge with left hand, right hand guard	**11.** ⇩ Step behind with left foot, close left hand	**12.** ⇩ Right hand punch

Wansu

13. ⇧ Pivot 180°, left hand leg block	**14.** ⇧ Right hand punch	**15.** ⇧ Step up right foot, right hand open arc sweep	**16.** ⇧ Gouge with left hand, right hand guard
17. ⇧ Step behind with left foot, close left hand	**18.** ⇧ Right hand punch	**19.** ⇩ Pivot 180°, left hand open arc sweep	**20.** ⇩ Reinforced right punch, left hand supporting
21. ⇩ Right foot straight kick	**22.** ⇩ Seiunchin stance, L hand forehead, R low	**23.** ⇩ Draw back with right foot, open both hands	**24.** ⇩ Set back into Seiunchin stance, close both hands

Wansu

25. ⇦ Pivot on left foot 270°, right hand push down	**26.** ⇨ Pivot 180°, left hand chop	**27.** ⇨ Right knee strike	**28.** ⇨ Right hand punch
29. ⇩ Pivot 90°, look to right	**30.** ⇦ Pivot 90°, right hand chop	**31.** ⇦ Left knee strike	**32.** ⇦ Left hand punch
33. ⇩ Pivot 90° to the left and draw feet together	**34.** ⇩ Step out with right foot, left hand punch on 45°	**35.** ⇩ Right hand punch on 45°	**36.** ⇩ Draw back foot up

Wansu

37. ⇩ Step out with left foot, right hand punch on 45°	**38.** ⇩ Left hand punch on 45°	**39.** ⇩ Draw feet together, stack hands on right hip	**40.** ⇨ Left foot side kick
41. ⇩ Stack hands on left hip	**42.** ⇦ Right foot side kick	**43.** ⇩ Left foot forward guard position	**44.** Step up with right foot, right elbow strike
45. ⇧ Draw back 180°, check with left knee	**46.** ⇧ Left foot straight kick	**47.** ⇩ Draw back 180°, check with right knee	**48.** ⇩ Right foot straight kick

Wansu

49. ⇩ Set down in right foot forward Seisan stance...	**50.** ⇩ Double hand chop outwards	**51.** ⇩ Left hand to belt, right hand guard	**52.** ⇩ Bring feet together
53. ⇩ Closing salutation	**54.** ⇩ Bow	**55.** ⇩ End of kata	

60

SEISAN BUNKAI DRILL 1

Original Kata moves *

Bow to each other. Defender in black, attacker in white

1

* Bunkai drill may not follow the Kata moves sequentially

Moves #2 & 4

Ready stance

2

SEISAN BUNKAI DRILL 1

3 Attacker throws right hand punch; push block with right hand…

4 … followed by left hand side block

5 Right hand straight punch to solar plexus

6 Attacker grabs right wrist (note: does not matter which hand he grabs with)

* Bunkai drill may not follow the Kata moves sequentially

Moves #5,6 & 7

SEISAN BUNKAI DRILL 1

7 Squat block; draw right hand through crook of left arm to peel attackers hand off. Simultaneously turn the back foot out and squat down into Seiunchin stance

* Bunkai drill may not follow the Kata moves sequentially

Moves #41 & 42

8 Completion of movement 7 above

SEISAN BUNKAI DRILL 1

9

10

9 Shift into opponent (shuffle forward) with reinforced left elbow strike to solar plexus (right hand over left fist)

10 Draw back into left foot forward cat stance, hands stacked on right hip

11 Step forward with left foot, left hand backfist to nose

11

* Bunkai drill may not follow the Kata moves sequentially

Moves #43, 43 & 44

64

SEISAN BUNKAI DRILL 1

Original Kata moves *

* Bunkai drill may not follow the Kata moves sequentially

Moves #44 & 45

12 While throwing the backfist, your side is open; attacker takes opportunity to throw punch (could be kick) to ribs

13 Drop left elbow for a block/strike to attacker's limb. End of drill – bow out

SEISAN BUNKAI DRILL 2

Bow in. Defender in black, attacker in white

1

Ready stance

2

* Bunkai drill may not follow the Kata moves sequentially

Moves #2 & 4

SEISAN BUNKAI DRILL 2

3 Attacker throws a side kick; draw back into cat stance and catch heel and toe

4 Left hand down, right hand up for ankle break

* Bunkai drill may not follow the Kata moves sequentially

Moves #70, 71 & 4

5 Reset into ready stance

SEISAN BUNKAI DRILL 2

6 Attacker reaches in for double hand choke/lapel grap

7 Block hands up and outward

8 Shuffle in for neck crank, using right hand to chin and left hand to back of neck

9 Right hand drops down to get a grip on attackers right sleeve, left hand prepares to...

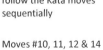

* Bunkai drill may not follow the Kata moves sequentially

Moves #10, 11, 12 & 14

SEISAN BUNKAI DRILL 2

10

11

10 ...Inverted ridge hand to attackers neck

11 Turn right hand over and get a grip on neck/collar/collar bone

12 Pull down with both hands, bringing attacker head near your right shoulder

12

* Bunkai drill may not follow the Kata moves sequentially

Moves #14, 15 & 16

SEISAN BUNKAI DRILL 2

Original Kata moves *

Reach over with left hand and grip attackers chin

13

* Bunkai drill may not follow the Kata moves sequentially

Moves #23 & 24

Complete "side block" motion for neck crank. Slow = control/takedown, fast = injury

14

NAIHANCHI BUNKAI DRILL 1

1 (Bow in) Ready Stance. Attacker in white, defender in black. Note defender's foot is inside attackers

2 Attacker grabs lapel with left hand, right hand rears back for punch

3 Hook-block punch with left arm ...

4 ... and cup behind attackers neck

* Bunkai drill may not follow the Kata moves sequentially

Moves: Bow, ready; #6, 6

NAIHANCHI BUNKAI DRILL 1

5 Elbow strike with right elbow, while restraining head with left hand

6 Right hand drops to grab attacks left hand, left forearm smash to crook of attacker's left elbow

7 Right cross kick to attacker's knee, bending him over further

8 Reach around with right hand to grab attacker's chin

* Bunkai drill may not follow the Kata moves sequentially

Moves #7, 8, 9 & 10

NAIHANCHI BUNKAI DRILL 1

9 Complete "leg block" motion for take down (slow = control / takedown, fast = injury)

* Bunkai drill may not follow the Kata moves sequentially

Moves #10 & 11

10 Gouge to neck. End of drill, bow out

NAIHANCHI BUNKAI DRILL 2

Original Kata moves *

1 (Bow in) Ready stance. Attacker in white, defender in black

2 Attacker throw knee strike to groin; defender turns knees in and double push-down block

3 Defender grabs attackers lapel with left hand

4 Right hand uppercut while left hand restrains

* Bunkai drill may not follow the Kata moves sequentially

Moves #1, 4, 15 & 16

4

NAIHANCHI BUNKAI DRILL 2

5

6

5 Right hand rears back for...

6 ... Back fist to nose

7 Right foot cross kick to knee while maintaining grip on lapel

7

* Bunkai drill may not follow the Kata moves sequentially

Moves #16, 17 & 18

NAIHANCHI BUNKAI DRILL 2

Original Kata moves *

8

9

8 Back fist across attacker's face with right hand

9 Sweep attacker's left foot out using defender's left foot

10 Hammer fist strike to side of attacker's jaw line

* Bunkai drill may not follow the Kata moves sequentially

Moves #19, 20 & 21

10

NAIHANCHI BUNKAI DRILL 2

11 Right hand grips collar/neck, both hands pull down

12 Right foot cross kick to over-extended left knee

* Bunkai drill may not follow the Kata moves sequentially

Moves #22, 23 & 24

13 Throw in direction of collapsed leg. End of drill, bow out

WANSU BUNKAI DRILL 1

Original Kata moves *

* Bunkai drill may not follow the Kata moves sequentially

Moves #2, 3, 4 & 29

1 Bow in. Attacker in white, defender in black. Note: for testing, student will assume role of defender

2 Get in position; attacker on right side with right hand on shoulder

3 Reinforced elbow to solar plexus

4 Begin parry motion to attackers right arm

78

WANSU BUNKAI DRILL 1

5 Completion of step four, grabbing sleeve and turning attacker to side

6 Knee to outer thigh, pressure point GB31 (peroneal nerve)

Moves #30, 31, & 32

* Bunkai drill may not follow the Kata moves sequentially

7 Straight punch to side with left hand

WANSU BUNKAI DRILL 1

8 Withdraw punch hand in preparation for...

9 Step up with left foot, elbow to floating ribs. Note: can also strike to attackers lockout out elbow

Moves #43, 44, & ready stance

* Bunkai drill may not follow the Kata moves sequentially

10 Reset in ready stance

80

WANSU BUNKAI DRILL 1

Original Kata moves *

11 Opponent throw kick to groin (can be straight kick or roundhouse), knee block

12 Without setting your foot down, return fire with a straight snap kick to attackers groin as soon as they set their foot down

Moves #47 & 48

* Bunkai drill may not follow the Kata moves sequentially

WANSU BUNKAI DRILL 2

Original Kata moves *

Bow to partner. Attacker in white, defender in black

1

Move #2

* Bunkai drill may not follow the Kata moves sequentially

Ready stance

2

WANSU BUNKAI DRILL 2

3 Attacker throws a left hand punch/haymaker to midsection/head

4 Defender parries and grabs with right hand, pulling in with a left hand punch

Moves #9, 10, & 11

* Bunkai drill may not follow the Kata moves sequentially

5 Defenders left hand then moves to the outside of attackers arm (Open arc sweep from chart 1), grabs, and pull to side exposing attackers ribs

WANSU BUNKAI DRILL 2

6 Right hand punch to floating rib

7 Both hands shift down to attacker wrist and pull down, loading attackers weight on front leg

Moves #12, 41, & 42

* Bunkai drill may not follow the Kata moves sequentially

8 Side kick with right foot to attackers front knee

WANSU BUNKAI DRILL 2

Pull/throw attackers arm wide with right hand, exposing attacker centerline

9

Moves #5 & 19

* Bunkai drill may not follow the Kata moves sequentially

10 Grab attackers lapel with left hand (Note: can use twisting grab here - starting with thumb down, grab, and then twist to the upright position which twists the gi up and takes out slack)

WANSU BUNKAI DRILL 2

11 Right hand punch to attacker nose

10b ALTERNATE MOVE TO #10: Cup behind neck with left hand

11b ALTERNATE MOVE TO #11: Right hand punch to face with neck restraint

12 Shift left hand down to grab attacker's sleeve at the bicep

* Bunkai drill may not follow the Kata moves sequentially

Moves #20, (19,20), 22

WANSU BUNKAI DRILL 2

13 Step deep between attackers legs with right foot into Seiunchin stance, reach between legs with right arm (be straight while under him, don't be bent forward at the waist)

Moves #24 & 25

* Bunkai drill may not follow the Kata moves sequentially

14 Lift attacker onto shoulders (must have his center of balance on your shoulders, lift with your legs); For the drill, this is the end (set gently back down), but for real life dump attacker onto ground

NON-TRADITIONAL KATAS

Custom 4-opponent Katas

Fill in each blank with the move you want to become proficient in. It can be any technique - the only qualification is that it works to stop the attack. Turn counterclockwise with each defense, simulating that:
1) Opponent to the front
2) Opponent to your left
3) Opponent behind you
4) Opponent to your Right

USE PENCIL: It is expected that your list will change often, as you learn new techniques or find that another technique is more effective for you.

Kata 1

1) Hook punch to head
⇒ _____
2) Lapel grab
⇒ _____
3) Punch to midsection
⇒ _____
4) Football tackle
⇒ _____

Kata 2

1) Uppercut to chin
⇒ _____
2) Knee to groin
⇒ _____
3) Wrist grab
⇒ _____
4) Bear hug back
⇒ _____

Kata 3

1) Guillotine
⇒ _____
2) Knife downward stab
⇒ _____
3) Knife thrust
⇒ _____
4) Stick swung at head
⇒ _____

Kumite Rock

General note: If you are spinning to kick with the right foot, spin clockwise. If kicking with the left foot, spin counterclockwise.

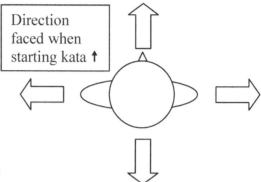

Part 1

1. Bow (⇧)
   Triple Strikes
2. Step out in RFF sparring stance, hands up (⇧)
3. Shuffle forward, RH backfist (⇧)
4. Step behind with left foot, right hand ridgehand (⇧)
5. Step out with right foot, groin strike (⇧)
6. *Pivot Upper Body (⇩)*
7. Shuffle forward, RH backfist (⇩)
8. Step behind with left foot, right hand ridgehand (⇩)
9. Step out with right foot, groin strike (⇩)
10. *Pivot upper body (⇧)*

   Low-high double kicks
11. Back (left) leg low kick, then high kick with setting foot down (⇧)
12. Set foot down in front, twisted around for... (⇧)
13. Right leg back kick. (⇩)
14. Back (right) leg low kick, then high kick with setting foot down (⇩)
15. Set foot down in front, twisted around for... (⇩)
16. Left leg back kick. (⇧)

Part 2

   All 4 weapons
17. Turn to the right (pivot on front (right) foot) (⇨)
18. Right hand backfist (⇨)
19. Left hand reverse punch (⇨)
20. Back foot (left) straight kick, set down in front turned backwards for... (⇨)
21. Right foot back kick. (⇦)

22. Left hand backfist (⇨)
23. Right hand reverse punch (⇨)
24. Back foot (right) straight kick, set down in front turned backwards for... (⇨)
25. Left foot back kick. (⇦)

Part 3

   Crescent Kicks
26. Turn to the right (pivot on front (right) foot) (⇩)
27. Right hand backfist, step up with feet together (⇩)

28. Right foot inside-out crescent kick (⇩)
29. Left hand straight punch (⇩)
30. *Pivot Upper Body (⇧)*
31. Left hand backfist, step up with feet together (⇧)
32. Left foot inside-out crescent kick (⇧)
33. Right hand straight punch (⇧)
34. *Pivot Upper Body (⇩)*

Jumping side kicks
35. Right foot jumping side kick
36. *Pivot Upper Body (⇧)*
37. Left foot jumping side kick
38. *Pivot Upper Body (⇩)*

Double jump kicks
39. Back leg first (left), low kick...
40. Jump, right leg high kick
41. Left hand chop down
42. *Pivot Upper Body (⇧)*
43. Back leg first (right), low kick...
44. Jump, left leg high kick
45. Right hand chop down
46. *Pivot Upper Body (⇩)*

Plain spinning Back Kicks
47. Bring back foot (left) around and set it down in front backward for... (⇩)
48. Right foot back kick (⇧)
49. Bring back foot (right) around and set it down in front backward for... (⇧)
50. Left foot back kick (LAND FACING FORWARD ⇧)

Foot Sweeps
51. Left hand backfist (⇧)
52. Back foot (right) sweep from right to left... (⇧)
53. Right foot back kick without setting foot down (⇩)
54. Step back with left foot into RFF Seisan stance (⇩)

55. Right hand backfist (⇩)
56. Back foot (left) sweep from left to right... (⇩)
57. Left foot back kick without setting foot down (⇧)
58. Step up with right foot into RFF Seisan stance (⇧)

Close
59. Draw back to attention (⇧)
60. Bow out (⇧)

Kumite Rock photos

1. Bow
2. Peace/Power
3. RFF Ready
4. Backfist
5. Ridge hand
6. Groin chop
7. Turn
8. Backfist
9. Ridge hand
10. Groin chop
11. Turn
12. Low roundhouse
13. ...Flip high
14. Set LF down
15. RF back kick
16. Ready

17. Low roundhouse   **18.** … Flip high   **19.** LF back kick,   **20.** set down

21. Turn   **22.** Back fist   **23.** Reverse P   **24.** Straight Kick

25. Set down…   **26.** Back kick   **27.** Set down   **28.** Back fist

29. Reverse P   **30.** Straight kick   **31.** Set down…   **32.** Back kick

33. Set down	**34.** Turn	**35.** LF up, backfist	**36.** Crescent kick
37. Reverse P	**38.** Turn	**39.** RF up, backfist	**40.** Crescent kick
41. Reverse P	**42.** Turn	**43.** Skipping…	**44.** Side kick
45. Ready	**46.** Skipping…	**47.** Side kick	**48.** Ready

49. Double...	**50.** Jump kick	**51.** LF chop	**52.** Turn
53. Double...	**54.** Jump kick	**55.** RF chop	**56.** Turn
57. Step up...	**58.** Back kick	**59.** Ready	**60.** Step up...
61. Back kick	**62.** Ready	**63.** Backfist	**64.** Foot sweep...

95

65. Back kick | **66.** Ready | **67.** Step back | **68.** Backfist
69. Foot sweep… | **70.** Back kick | **71.** Ready | **72.** Step up
73. Step back | **74.** Peace/power | **75.** Bow out

Stance Kata

1 Ready, bow	2 Salutation	3 Chart	4 Seisan
5 Seiunchin	6 Naihanchi	7 T-stance	8 Cat
9 Crane	10 Pivot, Seisan	11 Seiunchin	12 Naihanchi
13 T-stance	14 Cat	15 Crane	16 Pivot, Seisan

97

17 Step up

18 Seiunchin

19 Naihanchi

20 T-stance

21 Cat

22 Crane

23 Pivot, Seisan

24 Seiunchin

25 Naihanchi

26 T-stance

27 Cat

28 Crane

29 Pivot, Seisan

30 Step back

31 Chart

32 Bow out

Seison Manriki

Introduction

This kata was designed to use the Manriki-gusari in the Isshin-ryu kata Seison to teach traditional Manriki bunkai in a similar manner to Tatsuo's Kusanku-sai.

The Manriki shines when it comes to self-defense against a knife or bladed weapon, being used to "wrap-trap-throw." It is easily concealed, and the weapon can be easily improvised with a belt/purse strap/rope/power cord/etc.

Manriki history

Also known as Kusari-fundo or Ryofundogusari, among other names, the literal translation of Manriki-gusari is "Power of 10,000 chain," implying the leverage over an opponent that the use of the weapon gives. It is a chain anywhere from 1-3ft (usually 2ft), with a variety of weight shapes on the ends. It was developed/refined by Masaki Toshimitsu Dannoshin *(1689-1776),* one of the most skilled swordsmen of his day, as a bloodless weapon that could be used to defend the grounds of Edo castle *(keep in mind that the famous events of the 47 Ronin took place there in 1701).* The Manriki-gusari was later used as well by police during arrests, and was generally considered as a type of concealed self-defense weapon. Use of the Manriki-Gusari is a style unto itself; the original style is called "Masaki-Ryu," which branched out into other styles such as Hoen-ryu, Shuchin-ryu, Shindo-ryu, etc. You will often seen it referred to as a Ninja weapon, but this casts a false light on the Manriki - it was originally designed and used by samurai, and its use was later adopted by those in Ninjitsu. The samurai treated the Manriki with great respect, and often carried it in their sash as a backup weapon. While at home, it would be laid on a small plate where it could be near at hand.

References:
1. *Secrets of the samurai: a survey of the martial arts of feudal Japan*, Oscar Ratti, Adele Westbrook, Tuttle Publishing, 1991 page 317
2. *Classical weaponry of Japan: special weapons and tactics of the martial arts*, Serge Mol, Kodansha International, 2003 pages 125-136
3. *Spike and Chain: Japanese Fighting Arts*, Charles Gruzanski, Charles E. Tuttle Company, 1968 pages various

Manriki holds

- Held with one hand down the back of your leg
- Gathered in fist, ready to sling out
- Over arm (nunchucks)
- At side, one arm high one arm low
- In sleeve with end hanging out
- Around back, like you hands are at your belt
- Folded over and looped through belt
- Diagonally across the back (nunchucks)
- One arm out to side, other at chest

Seison Manriki Photos

Note: This kata assumes that the student already has a basic knowledge of Seison kata

Key:
RH= Right Hand   OH = Over Head   R = Right
LH = Left Hand   L = Left   SWW = Strike with weight

1. Bow	2. Wansu fist	3. LH Leg block	4. Sling out
5. LH Leg block	6. Swing up	7. L Side Block	8. R Side Block
9. L Side Block	10. Head Block	11. Eye Gouge	12. Guard

13. Leg Block

14. Head Block

15. Swing R-L

16. OH, to Back

17. Swing L-R

18. OH, to Back

19. Swing R-L

20. Guard

21. LH SWW

22. L Side Block

23. R block, kick

24. L Side Block

25. Stack, pivot

26. RH SWW

27. R Side Block

28. L Block, kick

29. Stack, pivot	**30.** LH SWW	**31.** L Side Block	**32.** R Side Block
33. R kick	**34.** Squat block	**35.** RH up guard	**36.** Swing down
37. Guard	**38.** Step across	**39.** R kick	**40.** Swing low L-R
41. Swing up	**42.** Guard	**43.** R Side Block	**44.** Squat Block

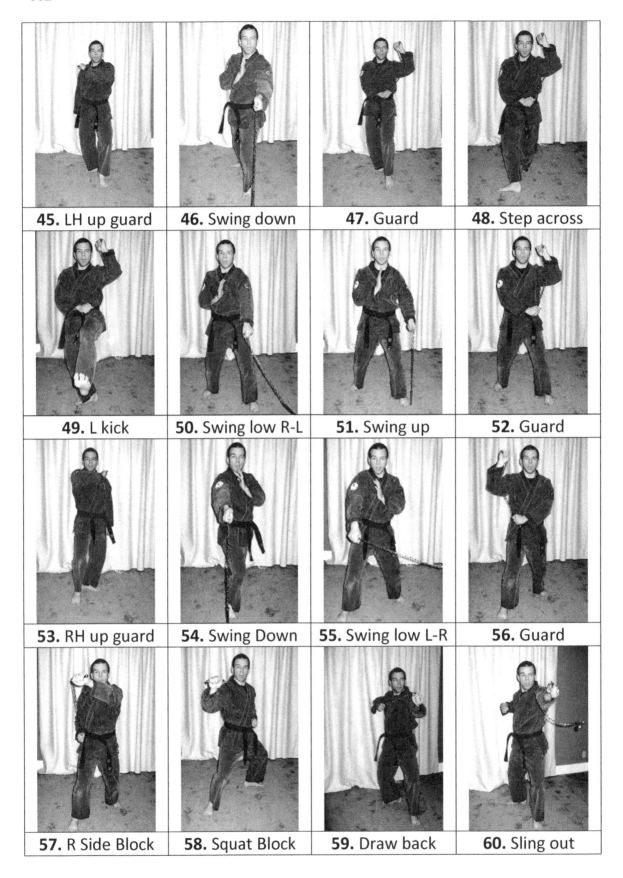

45. LH up guard	**46.** Swing down	**47.** Guard	**48.** Step across
49. L kick	**50.** Swing low R-L	**51.** Swing up	**52.** Guard
53. RH up guard	**54.** Swing Down	**55.** Swing low L-R	**56.** Guard
57. R Side Block	**58.** Squat Block	**59.** Draw back	**60.** Sling out

61. R kick	**62.** L Side Block	**63.** Back, wrap	**64.** Choke
65. Wipe Manriki	**66.** Over arm, bow		

Mini-weapons kata – <u>**Bo**</u>

Reagan 4/21/15

1. Bow in.	2. Bring bo up to ready, both hands upside doen	3. LFB, block across to left	4. Spin bottom end of bo under armpit, striking L-R w/other end
5. Bring bo to left hip in ready stance	6. Strike L-R with back end of bo…	7. Strike R-L with front end of bo	8. RFF in Seiunchin, upward groin strike
9. RF draw back for…	10. Forward thrust	11. Parry clockwise (your perspective)	12. Bow out

Mini-weapons kata – <u>Sai</u>

Jeff 3-9-17

1. Bow in with sai in right hand	2.Step up with Right foot, side block to right side	3. Flip out, strike to temple	4. Jab to solar plexus

5. Rake from left to right	6. Uppercut	7. Step up with right foot, elbow jab	8. Switch sai to left hand, turn side block with left foot forward

9. Flip out, strike to temple (moves 8-12 are a repeat of 2-6 using the other hand)	10. Jab to solar plexus	11. Rake from right to left	12. Uppercut. Switch sai to right hand, turn clockwise to front and bow out.

Mini-weapons kata – **Tonfa**

Jeff 3-14-17

1. Bow in with tonfa in right hand, ready stance	2.Step up with Right foot, head block	3. Flip out, strike to knee	4. Flip back, push-down block w/ L hand, punch to groin with tonfa

5. Step back, knee strike to rear	6. Switch tonfa to other hand, step up punch *	7. Step parallel, elbow strike with tonfa *	8. Head block/leg block **

9. Inside block (from left-to-right)**	10. Turn to front, bow out	* Image in mirror on wall, #6 & #7	**Image in mirror on wall, #8 & #9

Mini-weapons kata – **Kama**

Reagan 4/21/15

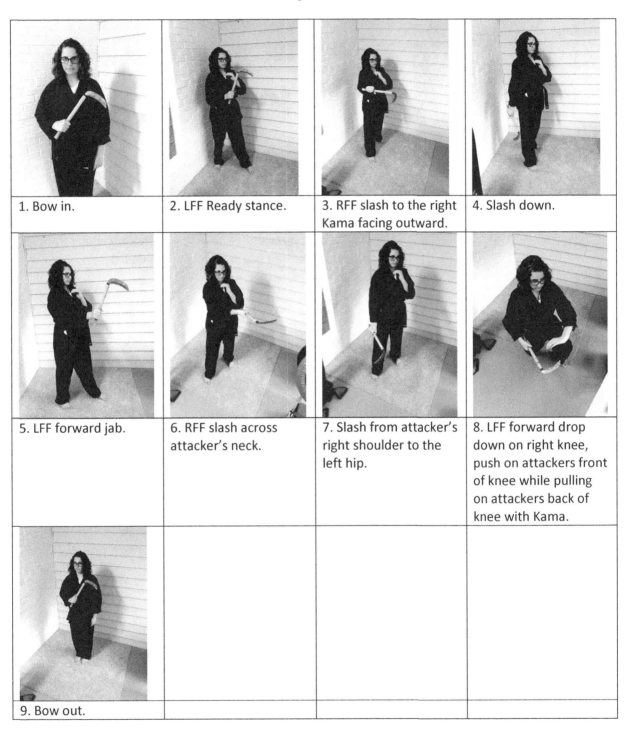

1. Bow in.	2. LFF Ready stance.	3. RFF slash to the right Kama facing outward.	4. Slash down.
5. LFF forward jab.	6. RFF slash across attacker's neck.	7. Slash from attacker's right shoulder to the left hip.	8. LFF forward drop down on right knee, push on attackers front of knee while pulling on attackers back of knee with Kama.
9. Bow out.			

Mini-weapons kata – **Kubaton**

Reagan 4/21/15

1. Bow in.	2. LFF Ready stance.	3. RFF Grab both ends of Kubaton and push to attacker's nose at pressure point.	4. RH groin strike with tip of Kubaton to attacker coming from behind.
5. RFF, Right hand strike across face from right to left.	6. Strike to temple from left to right.	7. LFF jab to throat.	8. RF sweeps attackers right leg clotheslining into a dump...
9. Transitioning into a Seiunchin stance.	10. Bow out.		

Mini-weapons kata – **Katana**

Parker 4/21/15

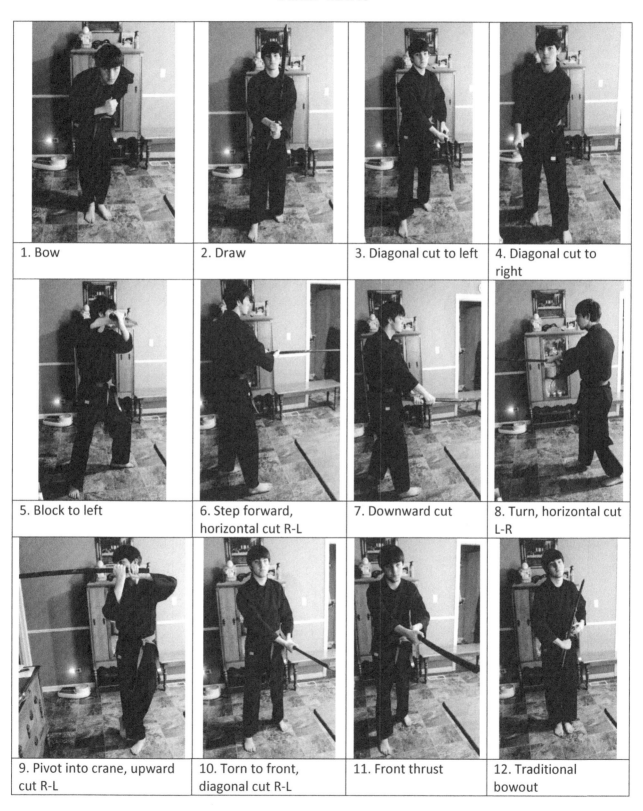

1. Bow	2. Draw	3. Diagonal cut to left	4. Diagonal cut to right
5. Block to left	6. Step forward, horizontal cut R-L	7. Downward cut	8. Turn, horizontal cut L-R
9. Pivot into crane, upward cut R-L	10. Torn to front, diagonal cut R-L	11. Front thrust	12. Traditional bowout

Mini-weapons kata – **<u>Yawara</u>**

Renae 4/21/15

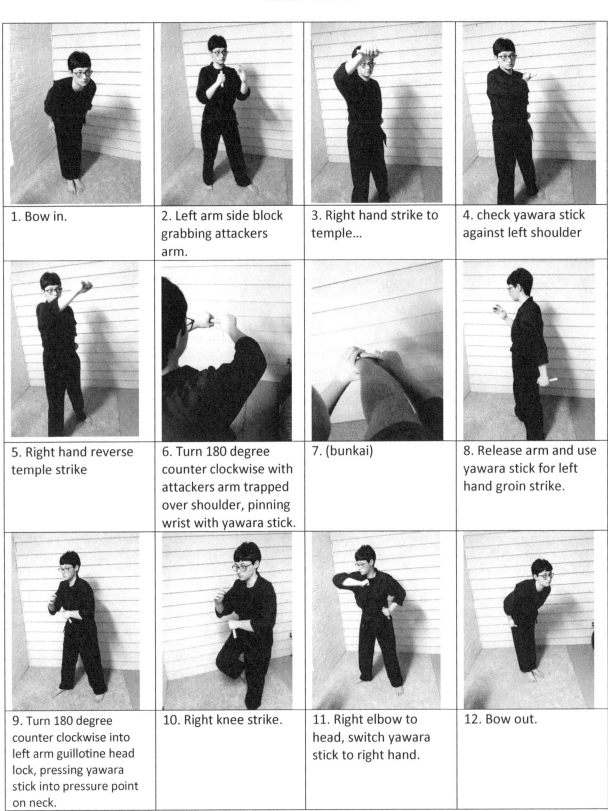

1. Bow in.	2. Left arm side block grabbing attackers arm.	3. Right hand strike to temple...	4. check yawara stick against left shoulder
5. Right hand reverse temple strike	6. Turn 180 degree counter clockwise with attackers arm trapped over shoulder, pinning wrist with yawara stick.	7. (bunkai)	8. Release arm and use yawara stick for left hand groin strike.
9. Turn 180 degree counter clockwise into left arm guillotine head lock, pressing yawara stick into pressure point on neck.	10. Right knee strike.	11. Right elbow to head, switch yawara stick to right hand.	12. Bow out.

Mini-weapons kata – <u>**Nunchucks**</u>

Brian Summers

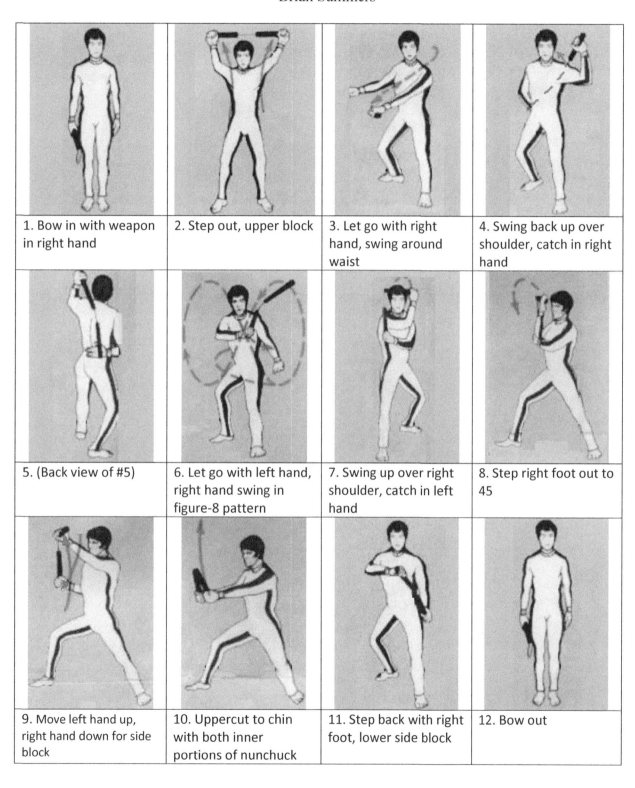

1. Bow in with weapon in right hand	2. Step out, upper block	3. Let go with right hand, swing around waist	4. Swing back up over shoulder, catch in right hand
5. (Back view of #5)	6. Let go with left hand, right hand swing in figure-8 pattern	7. Swing up over right shoulder, catch in left hand	8. Step right foot out to 45
9. Move left hand up, right hand down for side block	10. Uppercut to chin with both inner portions of nunchuck	11. Step back with right foot, lower side block	12. Bow out

Mini-weapons kata – <u>**Manriki**</u>

Renae 4/21/15

1. Bow in.	2. Right hand upward toss/sling, catch with left hand while still holding other end with right hand.	3. Step up left foot, left hand head block to block overhead downward attack.	4. Shuffle forward bringing manriki over attacker's neck, drawing into a right knee strike to groin.
5. Right foot step up, turn counter clockwise.	6. Step back with left foot into right foot forward seisan stance, double down block.	7. Release left hand manriki, left knee strike.	8. Right hammer fist to head.
9. Turn 180 degree left foot forward seisan striking attackers head with ball of manriki.	10. Right foot forward step up, right elbow strikes high.	11. Bow out.	

Grappling Kata
Leo Britt 2-26-12

Introduction
You and your opponent are standing trading punches. Your opponent is an experienced boxer, so you decide to take the fight to the ground to gain an advantage.

1. **Double Leg Takedown**
   a. Slip past a punch to get close to your opponent
   b. Drop to one knee and grab behind both of your opponent's ankles
      i. *Note: keep your face up an into opponents armpit to keep from getting in a headlock as you take him down.*
   c. Step up and drive with shoulder to send your opponent backwards

2. **Side mount**
   a. You are now standing and your opponent is on his back. You attempt to punch/kick your downed opponent, but he is keeping you off with kicks from the ground
      i. *Note: for a grappling match, it is better to go down with your opponent from the takedown into guard.*
   b. During one of your opponent's kicks, cross-grab his angle (e.g., grab his right ankle with your right hand)
   c. Pull to side (in example above, to right side) to get past opponents legs and drop to side mount

3. **Mount**
   a. Maintaining a tight side mount (knees and elbows against opponent's ribs and sides of head), slide knee over opponents stomach to mount position

4. **Flip positions**
   a. Opponent traps your arm (monkey grip) and leg (ankle hook) on one side
   b. Opponent bucks with hips while pressing with his free hand on your hip to roll you over, ending up on top in your guard

5. **Opponent stands up**
   a. Your opponent, not wishing to continue ground fighting, attempts to stand up
      i. *Note: opponent brings both feet close to your hips in order to stand straight up – very important*
   b. You clasp your hands behind his neck, attempting to keep him down

6. **Ankle hook takedown**
   a. Right as your opponent is about to break free from your clasp, perform the following movements simultaneously:
      i. Release your grip on opponent's neck and drop your hands to clasp behind his ankles
      ii. Release your feet from around opponent's waist and bring your feet to the front of your opponent's thighs / hip bones
   b. Thrust your feet forward and pull with your hands to send your opponent backwards
      i. *Note: This variation is for a tall opponent – otherwise it is better to just bring your knees together in front of your opponent's stomach for the takedown, then follow him over to end up in mount*

7. **Stand back up**

114

a. Bring your left foot up near your hip and plant it on the floor
b. Sit up and post on your right hand
c. Lift your body about an inch over the floor
d. Using your left foot and right hand as pivot points, swing your right leg under you and away from your opponent, planting it on the floor near your right hand
e. Stand up away from your opponent in seiuchin stance
f. During all of this, your opponent has gotten up as well – can get up just like you got up or something different
   i. *Note: This can be done on the opposite side as well; does not make a difference for this kata*

8. Go to clinch
a. You close the distance on your opponent and go to the clinch
b. You attempt to hook the front leg for a takedown, but are unable to get it
   i. *Note: It is always better to take your opponent down so that you land on top. However, you have just attempted to do that and your opponent will not go down, so the only thing left is to pull him into your guard (below)*

9. Pull into guard
a. With both your arms under his armpits, and cup-hooking the back of his shoulders with your hands, pull down so that you bend your opponent over
b. Sink straight down into a squat
c. From the squat, shoot backwards, pulling your opponent into your guard
   i. *Note: Shooting back is critical – it keeps you from taking a knee to the groin as you pull your opponent into your guard by keeping him stretched out*

10. Arm bar
a. Your opponent is in your guard, you have both hands behind his neck holding him down
b. Your opponent swims through between your arms and starts to post up with his hands against your chest
c. Maintaining your grip on the back of his neck with your left hand, shoot your right arm behind your opponents left leg and hook behind the knee in a bicep curl
d. Use your left hand under your opponents chin to push him away from you
e. Swing your left leg up and over your opponents head, while at the same time moving your right leg up the side of your opponents body
f. Cross your feet over your opponents back – both feet are now at your opponents left side
g. Use both hands to grab your opponents right wrist
h. Straighten your body and pull down with your arms to apply arm bar
   i. *Note: Keep your opponent's thumb pointed towards the ceiling while applying arm bar*
   ii. *Note: OPTIONAL: after applying arm bar, roll backwards and end the kata standing up*

~ End ~

Grappling Kata Photos

HISTORY

History of Isshinryu

Isshinryu was founded by one of the great karate masters, Tatsuo Shimabuku, and is derived from several of the other, older classical styles.

Master Tatsuo Shimabuku, began learning karate at the age of 14 and devoted the rest of his life to its study and teaching. For 26 years he studied the other styles, Shuri-te, Shorin-ryu and Goju-ryu, each one under the master of its style.

Master Shimabuku took the best of each style, improved it and founded Isshinryu. From Master Motobu, Master of Shuri-te, he took the kumite; from Master Kiyan, Master of Shorin, he took the Kata and added improvements; from Master Miyagi, Master of Goju, he took Sanchin, the basis of all Okinawan karate.

Isshinryu, with roots going back 500 years, is a postwar development, modernized to meet the needs of today's world. It was founded in the 50's and has been taught ever since to American Marines stationed in Okinawa.

Shimabuku's reputation throughout Okinawa had reached its peak when World War II struck the island. A business man as well as a karate teacher, the sensei's small manufacturing plant was completely demolished and he was bankrupt almost from the war's outset. He did his best to avoid conscription to the Japanese Army by escaping to the countryside where he worked as a farmer. As the situation grew more and more desperate for the Japanese and as the need to press the Okinawans into service became urgent, he was forced to flee.

As his reputation in karate spread among the Japanese, many soldiers began a thorough search as they wanted to study karate under him. The officers who finally caught up with him agreed to keep the secret of his whereabouts if he would teach them karate; it was in this manner that Master Shimabuku survived the war.

After the war, his business ruined and little chance of earning a living by teaching karate on the war-ravaged island, Master Shimabuku returned to farming and practiced karate privately for his own spiritual repose and physical exercise. Throughout Okinawa, he was recognized as the island's leading practitioner of both Shorin-ryu and Goju-ryu Karate.

In the early nineteen fifties, the sensei began to consider the idea of combining the various styles into one standard system. He could foresee the problems that were developing out of the differences among styles; he sagely concluded that a unification or synthesis of styles would enhance the growth of karate.

He consulted with the aged masters on the island, and with the heads of the leading schools. At first there was general agreement, but later his idea met resistance as the leaders of the various schools began to fear loss of identity and position. Sensei Shimabuku decided to go ahead on his own; thus Isshinryu Karate was born. On May 30,1975, Master Shimabuku passed away, leaving a legacy to the world of karate, and to all the future Isshinryu students.

The Isshinryu patch

First, let me say that Tatsuo was not a Christian. The Isshinryu patch has a lot of symbology in Okinawan religion (Shinto-ism). Since it has come over to the U.S, it has lost a lot of its origins and just become a symbol for Isshinryu. The main meanings behind the various parts of the patch are listed below. Due to its original origins, I prefer not to wear the patch (like Paul, not necessarily a sin, but do nothing that might offend others), but I do not have anything against others wearing or displaying it. A basic knowledge of what the patch symbolizes is required for blue belt.

Around the time he was formalizing Isshinryu, Tatsuo Shimabuku had a dream that was later incorporated into the Isshinryu patch. In the dream, a man approached Tatsuo. Tatsuo waved his open left hand in a gesture of peace. At the same time, Tatsuo kept his right hand closed into a fist in case this mysterious man meant harm. As the man went away, he left Tatsuo surrounded by a wall of flame. Tatsuo remained calm and used some water to extinguish the flames.

The Goddess

She is half woman, half serpent, representing both calm in the face of danger and fighting spirit. As Shimabuku did in his dream, she holds her left hand open and right hand closed, exhibiting peace and strength at once.

The Roiling Sea

The water's turbulence can signify the perils and challenges life puts to us, as well as our own internal struggles.

The Dragon

The most obvious interpretation of the dragon is as a reference to Shimabuku Tatsuo himself, since the word Tatsuo means "dragon."

The Three Stars

They may represent the great masters Kiyan, Miyagi and Motobu. They may also represent Shorinryu, Gojuryu and Kobudo

The Border

The orange color of the border is thought to signify the wall of flames.
The shape brings to mind Isshinryu's signature vertical fist.

The Sky

Its calmness carries the message that karate is to be used for defensive purposes only.

The shape

Usually an oval to represent Isshinryu's vertical fist, A.J. Advincula went even farther and made it into a true fist shape.

The Twenty Precepts
By Gichin Funakoshi

1. Karate-do begins with courtesy and ends with rei.

2. There is no first strike in karate.

3. Karate is an aid to justice.

4. First know yourself before attempting to know others.

5. Spirit first, technique second.

6. Always be ready to release your mind.

7. Accidents arise from negligence.

8. Do not think that karate training is only in the dojo.

9. It will take your entire life to learn karate, there is no limit.

10. Put your everyday living into karate and you will find "Myo" (subtle secrets).

11. Karate is like boiling water, if you do not heat it constantly, it will cool.

12. Do not think that you have to win, think rather that you do not have to lose.

13. Victory depends on your ability to distinguish vulnerable points from invulnerable ones.

14. The out come of the battle depends on how you handle weakness and strength.

15. Think of your opponents hands and feet as swords.

16. When you leave home, think that you have numerous opponents waiting for you.

17. Beginners must master low stance and posture, natural body positions are for the advanced.

18. Practicing a kata exactly is one thing, engaging in a real fight is another.

19. Do not forget to correctly apply: strength and weakness of power, stretching and contraction of the body, and slowness and speed of techniques.

20. Always think and devise ways to live the precepts of karate-do every day.

SEISAN

Found in over a score of styles, the kata Seisan (renamed Hangetsu "Half Moon" by Funakoshi) literally means "13" – possible the number of opponents or the number of individual techniques in the kata, those the original meaning is lost to history. It is unique in that is was taught in all three towns referred to as the birthplace of Okinawan Karate; Shuri, Naha, and Tomari (which also resulted in multiple variations of the kata). Isshinryu is unique in that it is the first kata taught, as opposed to many styles that save it for the advanced students. While from the Shorinryu lineage, the Isshinryu version shares many traits with the Goju-ryu kata. The early history is murky, but it is known that the kata originated in China, probably from Chinese Chuanfa, with a possible final tie in Yong Chun White Crane from Fuzhou (around mid-1500's).

Isshinryu	Tatsuo Shimabuku 1908-1975
Shorinryu	Chotoku Kyan 1870-1945
Shuri-te	Sōkon Matsumura 1809-1901
Te	Kanga Sakugawa 1733-1815
Ch'uan Fa	Takahara Peichin 1683-1760

SEIUNCHIN

There is no true literal translation of Seiunchin's meaning. Some believe the meaning is "Storm within the calm." The standard kanji of Seiunchin means "to control and pull in battle." It is one of two Gojuryu katas in Isshinryu, the other being Sanchin. Seiunchin is unusual in that is relies only on hand techniques, with no kicks. While the lineage below is generally accepted, it is suspected that Seiunchin existed in Okinawa before this lineage, though Kanryu went to China to basically get the kata "from the source."

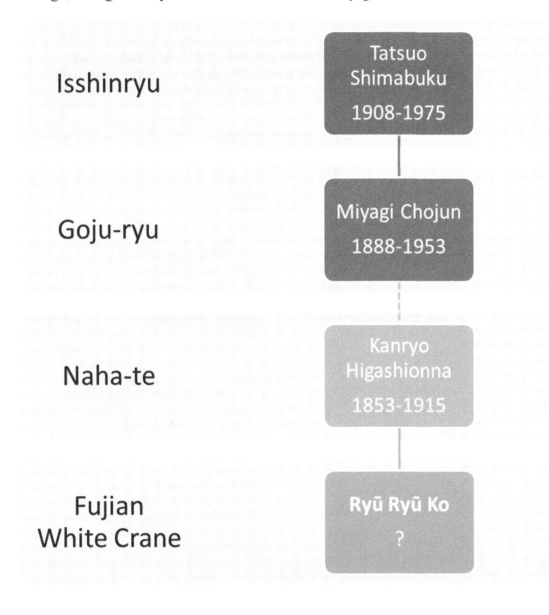

Isshinryu — Tatsuo Shimabuku 1908-1975

Goju-ryu — Miyagi Chojun 1888-1953

Naha-te — Kanryo Higashionna 1853-1915

Fujian White Crane — Ryū Ryū Ko ?

NAIHANCHI

Naihanchi (meaning "Internal Divided Conflict") which was re-named Tekki ("Iron Horse") by Gichin Funakoshi, was originally a much longer kata. It is generally accepted that Anko Itosu split the kata into three segments, Tekki Shodan, Tekki Nidan, and Tekki Sandan, though it is possible that he only split it in two and created the third portion himself. The Naihanchi of Isshinryu (originally learned through Kyan) is the first portion, Tekki Shodan, and is one of the katas least changed by Tatsuo. Choki Motobu was so adamant about this kata that it was even rumored Tekki-Shodan was the only kata he knew (which was false). Known for starting fights to test his fighting skills, Choki credited the kata with containing all that one needs to know to become a proficient fighter. It appears that Itosu introduced the pigeon-toed stance (Naihanchi-Dachi), which Motobu criticized, his own stance being toes forward (Kiba-Dachi). There is some uncertainty about who (or both) Matsumura learned the kata from, but it usually accepted that it has its roots in Chinese (Chuan Fa/White crane) martial arts. It is one of the most wide-spread katas in karate.

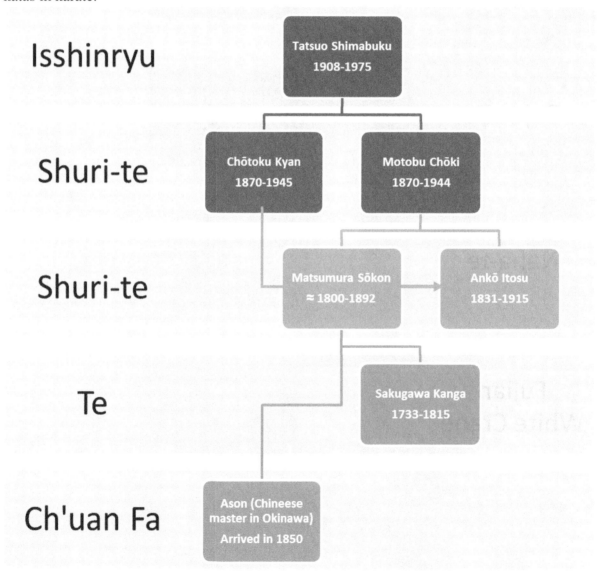

WANSU

Wansu (originaly Wanchu) has been translated by various sources as "Excellent Wrist", "Hidden Fist", "Wang's Series (or Form)", and refers to the name Wang, the leader of a large ambassadorial mission from China sent by the Qing government in 1683 to the village of Tomari. A poet, calligrapher, diplomat, and martial artist in the Shaolin tradition of Fujian White Crane, he is often credited with teaching chu'an fa to the gentry of Tomari. The Wanshū kata was either a creation of Wang's, or composed by his students and named in tribute to him. Wanshu was renamed Empi by Gichin Funakoshi in the 1920's when he brought the kata to Japan. There are two main versions of Wanshu – Matsumura lineage and Itosu lineage. The Itsou version (learned by Funakoshi) includes several changes, including a jump in the kata. (Wang Ji---Gusukama of Tomari---Itosu Ankoh---Gichin Funakosh) **Note:** Kosaku taught Kyan the kata Chinto, but it was his student Maeda that taught Kyan Wanshu.

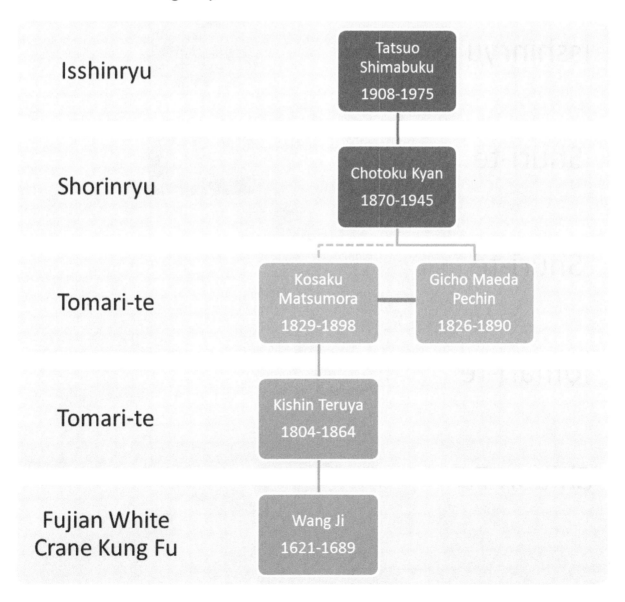

CHINTO

Legand states that a Chineese sailer (possible a pirate) named either Annan or Chinto who wreaked on the Okinawan coast. To survive, Chintō kept stealing from the crops of the local people. Matsumura Sōkon, a Karate master and chief bodyguard to the Ryūkyūan king, was sent to defeat Chintō. In the ensuing fight, however, Matsumura found himself equally matched by the stranger, and consequently sought to learn his techniques in exchange for amnesty. There are two distinct version of Chinto – the Shuri-te version and the Tomari-te version. Sōkon is said the have modified/stylized the kata to his preferences. While Sōkon was Kyan's primary teacher, Kyan's kata is said to almost exactly match the version taught by Kōsaku. When Gichin Funakoshi brought Karate to Japan, he renamed Chintō (meaning approximately "fighter to the east") to Gankaku (meaning "crane on a rock").

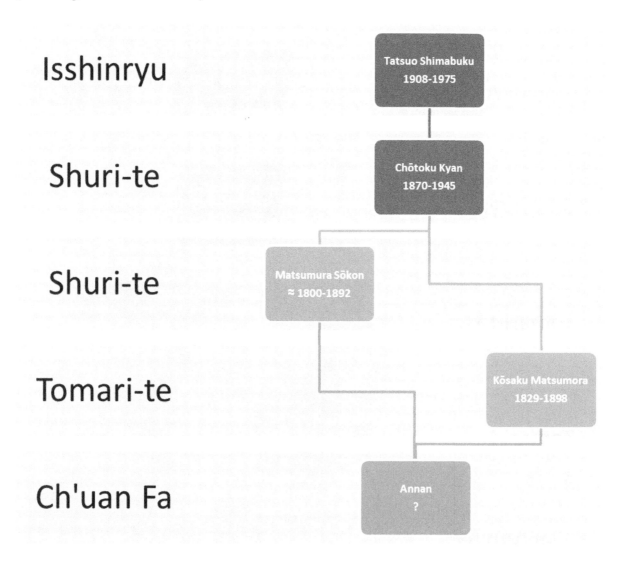

Isshinryu

Shuri-te

Shuri-te

Tomari-te

Ch'uan Fa

Tatsuo Shimabuku
1908-1975

Chōtoku Kyan
1870-1945

Matsumura Sōkon
≈ 1800-1892

Kōsaku Matsumora
1829-1898

Annan
?

KUSANKU

Kūsankū learned the art of Ch'uan Fa in China from a Shaolin monk. He was thought to have resided (and possibly studied martial arts) in the Fukien province for much of his life.[5] Around 1756, Kūsankū was sent to Okinawa as an ambassador of the Qing Dynasty.[6] He resided in the village of Kanemura, near Naha City. During his stay in Okinawa, Kūsankū instructed Kanga Sakukawa. Sakugawa trained under Kūsankū for six years. After Kūsankū's death (around 1762), Sakugawa developed and named the Kusanku kata in honor of his teacher.

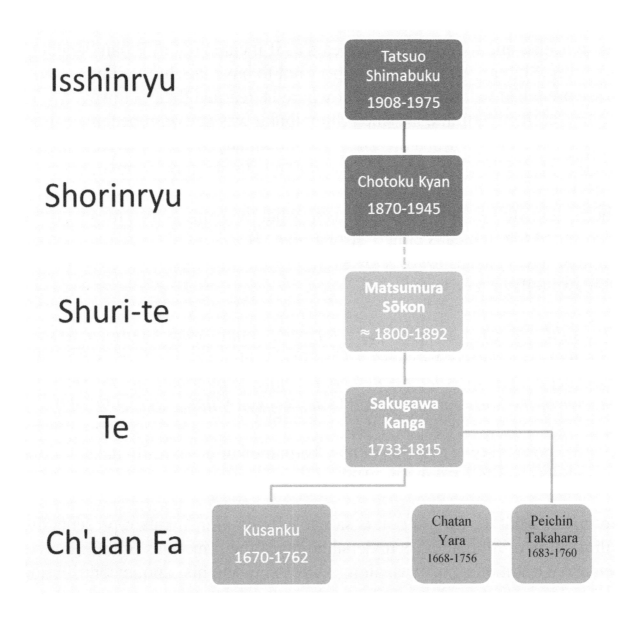

Sunsu

This kata was created by Shimabuku Tatsuo, although it is still unclear as to exactly when he created it (late 1940s?). It is often described as a combination of techniques and principles from the other seven Isshinryu karate kata. However, there are elements of other kata as well, such as Useishi (Gojushiho) and Passai that Shimabuku is thought to have learned under Kyan.

There is also one sequence that appears as if it came out of Pinan Sandan. However, Shimabuku's teachers appear not to have taught the Pinan kata, so we are faced with the problem of where he learned them. However, looking at the timeframe in which Shimabuku was active, it becomes clear that he could have learned the Pinan just about anywhere, or even just taken the technique via observing the Pinan kata being performed.

There seems to be some confusion as to what the name Sunsu means. It has been stated that it means either "strong man" (Uezu, et al, 1982) or "son of old man" (Advincula, 1998). However, a recent newspaper article from Okinawa tells us a different story:

"It is said that when Shimabuku performed Sanchin kata, he appeared so solid that even a great wave would not budge him, like the large salt rocks at the beach, and his students nicknamed him "Shimabuku Sun nu Su" (Master of the Salt) out of respect." (sic, Ryukyu Shinpo-sha, 1999, p.9)

Another possibility is that Sunsu may be named after a family dance of the Shimabuku family (Advincula, 1999).

No matter what the meaning, it is safe to say that Sunsu kata represents the culmination of Shimabuku's understanding of the principles of the defensive traditions, and was, along with Isshinryu, his unique contribution to the classical art of Okinawa karatedo.

Credit: http://www.sfisshinryu.com/2012/01/07/sunsu-%E3%82%B9%E3%83%B3%E3%82%B9%E3%82%A6-kata/

SANCHIN

Sanchin has been translated as "three battles/conflicts/wars" is usually interpreted as the battle to unify the mind, body, and spirit; alternatively, three opponents, three sets of techniques, lower body/upper body/ breathing, and so forth. It is one of two Gojuryu katas in Isshinryu, the other being Seiunchin. Some Gojoryu styles later use closed fists instead of the gouges, which was adopted by Miyagi. Often performed during tests/demonstrations with "Shime," or strikes/pushes to test balance an posture. It is common belief that the kata is intended as a form of strengthening for the karate student, building muscle and teaching the tightening to withstand a punch using principles of isometric tension. It is considered a foundational kata to many styles.

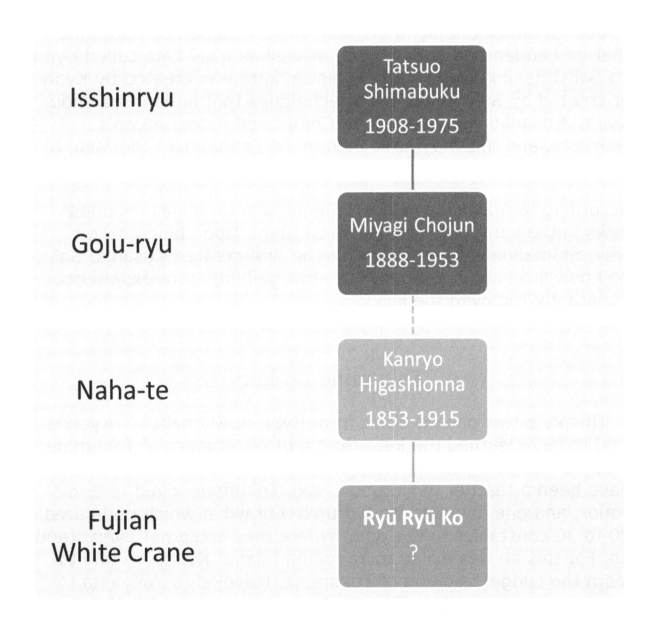

Isshinryu — Tatsuo Shimabuku 1908-1975

Goju-ryu — Miyagi Chojun 1888-1953

Naha-te — Kanryo Higashionna 1853-1915

Fujian White Crane — Ryū Ryū Ko ?

History of Weapon Katas

Credit: http://www.hgweb.nl/isshinryu/articles/kobudo.htm

Kusanku-sai

This kata was created by Shimabuku himself, based upon the Kusanku kata he had learned from Kyan. The following information was gleaned from a personal communication from A. J. Advincula (1998), who studied with Shimabuku in Okinawa. Before studying with Taira Shinken in the late 1950s and early 1960s, Shimabuku only knew the cudgel tradition of Tokumine that he had learned under Kyan, as well as a sai kata called Kyan no Sai. It is unknown whether this sai kata was created by Kyan or created by Shimabuku from techniques that he learned under Kyan. Kusanku was, along with Chinto and Passai, Kyan's specialty, and this may have influenced Shimabuku's decision to create a sai kata from this form.

According to Advincula (1998), Shimabuku originally included kicks in the kata, but later removed them. Upon being asked why, Shimabuku stated that when he first created Kusanku Sai, he knew little about kobudo, but after gaining more experience apparently removed the kicks.

Tokumine-no-kun

This kata was passed down from Kyan to Shimabuku. Kyan is said to have learned the kata from a direct student of Tokumine Peichin. According to the story, Tokumine Peichin was said to have been a teacher of Motobu Choki. Tokumine loved to drink liquor, and one day got into a drunken brawl in which he injured 20 to 30 constables to the point where they could not even stand up. For this he was exiled to Yaeyama Island. Kyan, wishing to learn the cudgel tradition of Tokumine, traveled to Yaeyama to seek out his instruction. Upon arriving, Kyan learned that Tokumine had already passed away, but had taught his kata to the old man who acted as the landlord of the place where Tokumine had lived. It was from the landlord that Kyan had actually learned this form. (Jahana, 1978)

Uezu Angi stated that Shimabuku studied this kata from Kyan, but later relearned it from Taira (Uezu, 1997). This author, however, has found no evidence to date that Taira ever taught or even knew this kata. It is one possibility that Shimabuku studied Tokumine no Kon under Kyan, but later when re-modifying the kata to fit his vision of kobudo, may have been influenced by Taira's method of utilizing the bo.

Urashi-bo

This kata came directly from Taira, and was modified by either Shimabuku or Taira. This kata is called Urasoe no Kon in Taira's syllabus, and can be found in Inoue's series. Urasoe is the standard Japanese pronunciation of the name whereas Urashi is the old Okinawan pronunciation. According to Nakamoto (1983) Taira supposedly learned this kata from Mabuni Kenwa (1889-1952), founder of Shitoryu, which went on to become one of the "big four" styles of modern Japanese karate do. Mabuni gained most of his influence from the likes of Itosu Anko (1831-1916), Higaonna Kanryo (1852-1915), Aragaki Seisho (1840-1920), etc.

By sheer coincidence, Mabuni's karate, like that of Shimabuku, is a unique blend of the various kata traditions that were formerly practiced in and around the three main "karate areas" i.e. the Shuri, Tomari, and Naha districts.

Chatanyara-no-sai

This kata was also passed down by Taira, who is said to have learned it from Kamiya Jinsei. It was either created by a master called Chatan Yara or based upon his teachings. Yara was, according to Nakamoto (1983), a karateka who lived before Bushi Matsumura (1809-1901), and studied under Kusanku who came from China in 1762. He also states that Yara, who held the title

Peichin, lived during the time of King Sho Boku who reigned from 1752-1795, and held a stipend of land in Chatan, where he carried out the last years of his life. This kata can also be found in Inoue's series.

Shishi-no-kun

This kata was quite difficult to trace the origins of. The kanji (Sino-Japanese ideogram) for this kata in Isshinryu are usually written in a manner that is very similar to the name for a separate bojutsu tradition called Shushi no Kon. However, upon witnessing these two kata being performed, one can immediately see that they are two different kata.
In Matayoshi Kobudo there appears a kata named Shishi no Kon. However, the form is quite different from Isshinryu's Shishi no Kon, and the kanji for the Matayoshi kata are the same as the kata that in the Taira lineage this is pronounced Soeishi no Kon (Matayoshi, 1996).

Observing this, this author immediately looked up the kata Soeishi no Kon in Inoue's series. The similarities are striking. Upon further investigation, it was found that Shishi is the Okinawan pronunciation of the kanji. Based upon these observations, this author concluded that the Shishi no Kon no Dai of Shimabuku Tatsuo is based upon the Soeishi no Kon Dai of Taira. As with Chatan Yara no Sai, Taira learned this kata from Kamiya Jinsei. As with the other Taira-based kata within the Isshinryu Kobudo curriculum, it is unclear whether Shimabuku or Taira made these changes, or if it was a collaborative effort.

This kata is named after the Soeishi family, who, according to Miyagi (1987) were the instructors to the King. The kata itself, again according to Miyagi (1987) uses the bo in a horizontal manner, different from other cudgel traditions. According to Nakamoto (1983), this kata, along with the previously mentioned Shushi no Kon, as well as Choun no Kon, are said to have been developed by a certain Soeishi Sensei, who was a high ranking lord in Shuri.

Hamahiga-no-tuifa

This was another kata taught to Shimabuku by Taira. In the now-famous 1966 film taken of Shimabuku during his second and last visit to the United States, this kata is often denoted as Chie-fa in English. However, this is nothing more than a misspelling of a misspelling.

It is said that Shimabuku always referred to the weapon as tuifa. On the 1966 film, the katakana syllabary for this kata reads Tsuifa, an innocent misspelling, apparently made my the Japanese translator, which was then misspelled again as Chie-fa in English.

According to Perkins (1998) Tokumura Kensho, a direct student of Shimabuku, stated in an interview that Shimabuku never taught the kata on the film in Okinawa. There is speculation that this kata is what bits and pieces Shimabuku remembered from the longer, older Hama Higa no Tuifa as taught by Taira.

This longer, older version can be found in Inoue's series as well as in Taira's own book. On the film, one can clearly see him fumbling for movements and techniques. However, there are still Isshinryu groups in the United States and elsewhere who still refer to this kata as Chie-fa no Tonfa, apparently because that's what it says on the film.

The following account of Hama Higa Peichin is a summary of an essay written by Taira Shinken, and can be found in the 1998 republication of his 1964 Ryukyu Kobudo Taikan (pages 183-184). Hama Higa accompanied King Sho Shin and Prince Nago Chogen on their trip to Edo, where he played a game of go with the famous Japanese master Hon'inbo Dosaku on 17 April, 1682. It is also said that with the permission of Shimazu Hidehisa of Satsuma, Hama Higa also performed Toudi (Karate) and Saijutsu in front of the 4th Shogun Tokugawa Tsunayoshi. This sai kata later became known as Hama Higa no Sai, and is still practiced in Okinawa kobudo today. (Taira, 1998)

Map of Isshinryu

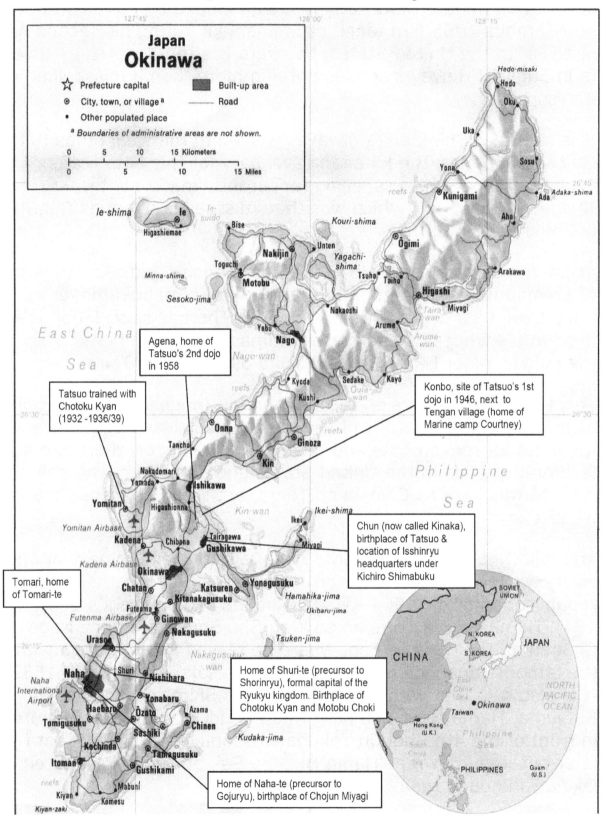

Isshinryu Timeline - pg 1

Date	Tatsuo Teachers	Tatsuo	Isshinryu	Tatsuo Students	Historical Backdrop
1869					
1870	Dec.1870 Birth of Chotoku Kyan born				1870 Napolean III overthrown
1871	April 5, 1870 Birth of Motobu Choki				
1872					
1873					
1874					
1875					
1876					
1877					
1878					
1879					1879 Okinawa becomes part of Japan
1880					
1881					
1882					
1883					
1884					
1885					
1886					
1887					
1888		April 25, 1988 Birth of Chojun Miyagi			
1889					
1890	At 20, Kyan begins training w/Matsumora & Oyadomari				
1891					
1892					
1893					
1894					
1895					
1896					
1897	June 12, 1987 Birth of Taira Shinken				1898-1901 Boxer rebellion takes place
1898					
1899					
1900					

Isshinryu Timeline - pg 2

Date	Tatsuo Teachers	Tatsuo	Isshinryu	Tatsuo Students	Historical Backdrop
1901					1901 Karate in Okinawan schools by Itosu Ankoh
1902					
1903					
1904					
1905					
1906					
1907					
1908		Sep. 19, 1908 Birth of Tatsuo Shimabuku			
1909					
1910					
1911					
1912					
1913					
1914					1914 WW1 begins
1915	1915; Miyagi studies in Fujian, China.				
1916					
1917					
1918					
1919					1919 Treaty of Versailles signed
1920		At 12, begins to study under his uncle Shinko			
1921	1921; Motobu Choki moved to Japan				
1922					
1923					
1924					
1925	1925; Motobu boxing match				
1926					
1927					
1928					
1929	Late 1929 Miyagi founds Gojoryu				Oct. 24, 1929 Stock market crash
1930				Sep 3, 1930 Birth of Harold Long	
1931				Sep 22, 1931 Birth of Steve Armstrong	
1932		1932; Begins to study under Chotoku Kyan			
1933				Dec 17, 1933 Birth of Harold Mitchum	
1934					
1935					
1936					Oct. 25, 1936 Meeting of masters in Naha
1937	1940; Taira opens Kobudo dojo in Naha				
1938				April 5, 1938 Birth of Don Nagle	
1939					

Isshinryu Timeline - pg 3

Date	Tatsuo Teachers	Tatsuo	Isshinryu	Tatsuo Students	Historical Backdrop
1940					
1941	1941 Motobu Choki moved back to Okinawa	1941: Begins to study under Choki Motobu (1yr)			
1942					
1943					
1944	April 5, 1944 Death of Motobu Choki	Cir. 1945; Begins to study under Chojun Miyagi			1 April-22 June 1945; Battle of Okinawa (1/4 all civilians die)
1945	Sep.20 1945 Death of Chotoku Kyan				
1946					
1947					
1948					
1949					
1950				Long trains w/Tatuo 1957-59 (1yr & 7mo)	June 25 1950 July 27 1953 Korean war
1951					
1952					
1953	Oct. 8, 1953 Death of Chojun Miyagi				
1954					
1955	1955; Tiara founds Kobudo society	1955; Tatsuo has dream that is basis of Isshinryu patch	Jan 15, 1956 Isshinryu Style founded	Nagle trains w/Tatsuo 7/11/56-9/9/57 (1yr & 2.5mo)	
1956					
1957				Mitchum trains w/Tatsuo 2/19/58-5/1/59 10/1959-11/1960 4/1961-11/1964 (5yr & 10 mo)	
1958		1958; Moves dojo from Chan to Agena — Cir. 1958+; Begins to study under Taira Shinken			
1959					
1960			Additional Kobudo weapons added to Isshinryu — 1961 AOKA founded	June 10, 1961 Tatsuo reciends high promotions	
1961					
1962					
1963					
1964		1964; 1st visit to the USA			
1965					
1966				1966; Tatsuo awards 8th dan to Mitchum, Nagle, Armstrong, & Long — 1966; 2nd visit to the United States	
1967					
1968					July 1, 1969 Apollo 11 on moon
1969					
1970	Sep. 3, 1970 Death of Taira Shinken			Early 1972 Retirement	
1971					
1972					
1973					

Isshinryu Timeline - pg 4

Date	Tatsuo Teachers	Tatsuo	Isshinryu	Tatsuo Students	Historical Backdrop
1974			1974; AOKA renamed IWKA	74; Mitchum retires from Marines; opens dojo	April 30, 1975 End of Vietnam War
1975		May 30, 1975 Death of Tatsuo Shimabuku			
1976					
1977			1977; Formation of the UIKA		
1978					
1979			1979 Formation of the IIKA		
1980				1980; Long creates the IHOF	
1981					
1982					
1983					
1984					
1985					
1986					
1987					
1988					
1989					Nov 9, 1989 Fall of Berlin Wall
1990					Aug 2 1990
1991					Feb 28 1991; Gulf war
1992					
1993					
1994					
1995					
1996					
1997					
1998				Oct 12, 1998 Death of Harold Long	
1999				Aug 23, 1999 Death of Don Nagle	
2000					
2001					Nov 11 2001 9/11 attacks
2002					
2003					
2004					
2005					
2006				Nov 15, 2006 Death of Armstrong	
2007					
2008					
2009					
2010					
2011					
2012					

Lineage of Isshinryu
Quick reference (non-comprehensive) with focus on TN area
Scott Britt 5/9/13, Revision 1

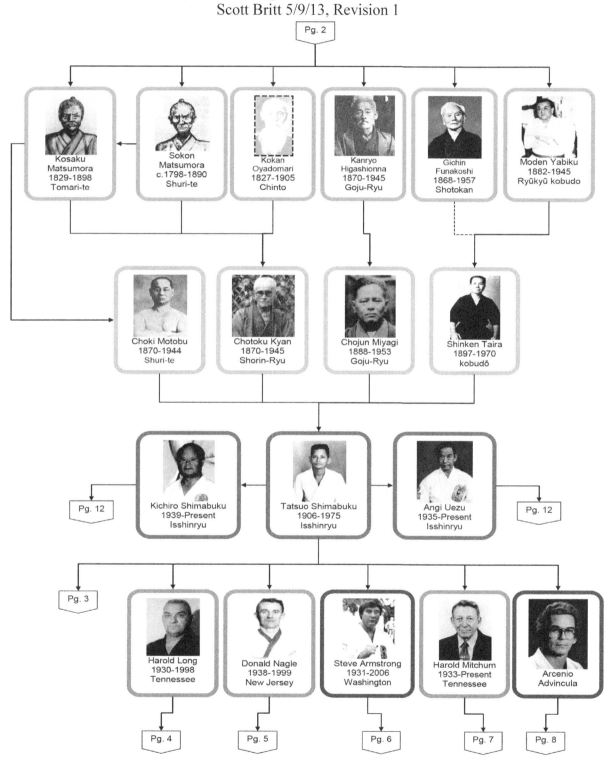

Pg. 2

Kosaku Matsumora
1829-1898
Tomari-te

Sokon Matsumora
c.1798-1890
Shuri-te

Kokan Oyadomari
1827-1905
Chinto

Kanryo Higashionna
1870-1945
Goju-Ryu

Gichin Funakoshi
1868-1957
Shotokan

Moden Yabiku
1882-1945
Ryūkyū kobudo

Choki Motobu
1870-1944
Shuri-te

Chotoku Kyan
1870-1945
Shorin-Ryu

Chojun Miyagi
1888-1953
Goju-Ryu

Shinken Taira
1897-1970
kobudō

Pg. 12

Kichiro Shimabuku
1939-Present
Isshinryu

Tatsuo Shimabuku
1906-1975
Isshinryu

Angi Uezu
1935-Present
Isshinryu

Pg. 12

Pg. 3

Harold Long
1930-1998
Tennessee

Donald Nagle
1938-1999
New Jersey

Steve Armstrong
1931-2006
Washington

Harold Mitchum
1933-Present
Tennessee

Arcenio Advincula

Pg. 4

Pg. 5

Pg. 6

Pg. 7

Pg. 8

NOTE: Any omissions are due solely to a lack of knowledge about that particular branch of Issinryu, and are not intentional. The order of pages is not based on any type of rank or rating, but was determined only by who was being added next as the chart was created.

140

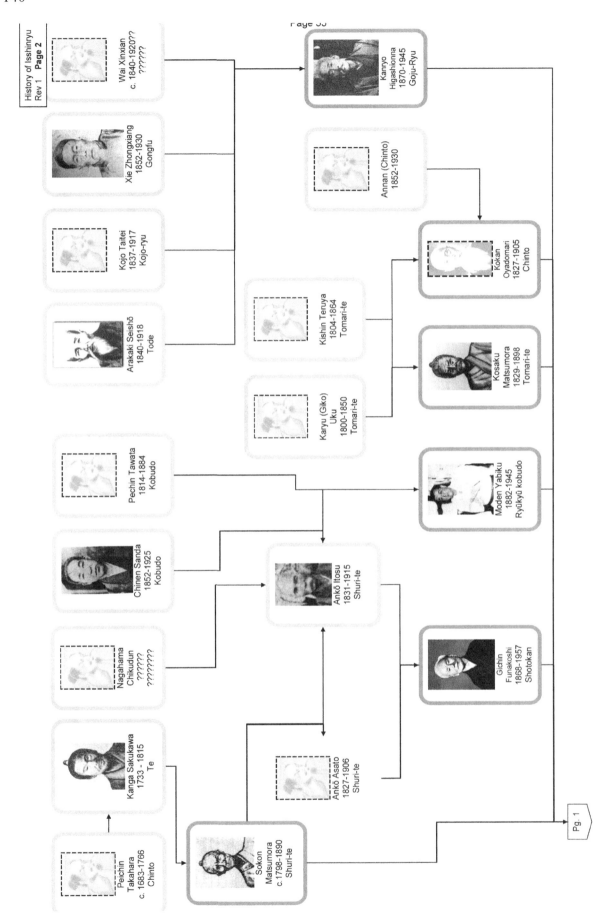

History of Isshinryu Rev 1 **Page 2**

Wai Xinxian c. 1840-1920?? ?????

Page 55

Kanyo Higashionna 1870-1945 Goju-Ryu

Xie Zhongxiang 1852-1930 Gongfu

Annan (Chinto) 1852-1930

Kojo Taitei 1837-1917 Kojo-ryu

Kokan Oyadomari 1827-1905 Chinto

Arakaki Seishō 1840-1918 Tode

Kishin Teruya 1804-1864 Tomari-te

Kosaku Matsumora 1829-1898 Tomari-te

Karyu (Giko) Uku 1800-1850 Tomari-te

Pechin Tawata 1814-1884 Kobudo

Moden Yabiku 1882-1945 Ryūkyū kobudo

Chinen Sanda 1852-1925 Kobudo

Ankō Itosu 1831-1915 Shuri-te

Nagahama Chikudun ?????-???????

Gichin Funakoshi 1868-1957 Shotokan

Kanga Sakukawa 1733 - 1815 Te

Ankō Asato 1827-1906 Shuri-te

Peichin Takahara c. 1683-1766 Chinto

Sokon Matsumora c.1798-1890 Shuri-te

Pg. 1

141

History of Isshinyu
Rev 1   **Page 3**

Tatsuo Shimabuku
1906-1975

Pg. 1

S. Shimabuku pg 11

Arcenio Advincula

Pg. 8

Harry G. Smith pg 20

Jim Larocco pg 12

Harry Acklin
8th - Deceased

Garry Baker
5th - Deceased

John Bartusevics
8th

Ed McGrath pg 5

Donald Bohan (this pg)

Don Nagle pg 5

Richard Bell
6th - Deceased

Phil Little pg 19

Russell Best

William Blonde

Donald Bohan

Pg. 18

Ralph Bove

George Breed

Bob Bremer

Chris Chase

Julie Tittl Pg 20

Charles Conners

Toby Cooling

Dennis Bootle pg 5

Aubrey "Bud" Ewing

Barry Smith

Diane Cooling

CONTINUED ON PAGE 10

142

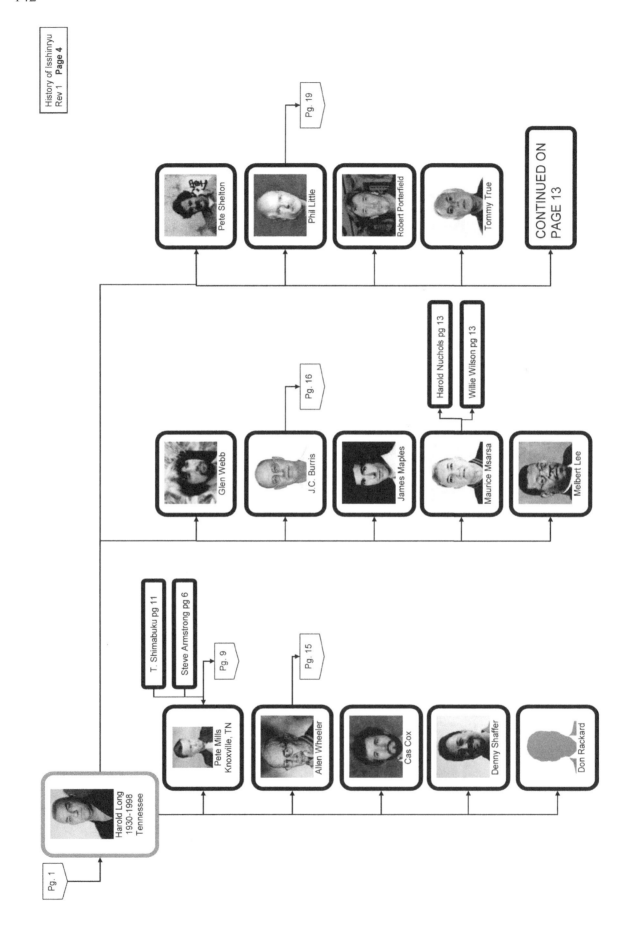

Pg. 19

Pete Shelton

Phil Little

Robert Porterfield

Tommy True

CONTINUED ON PAGE 13

Harold Nuchols pg 13

Willie Wilson pg 13

Pg. 16

Glen Webb

J.C. Burris

James Maples

Maurice Msarsa

Melbert Lee

T. Shimabuku pg 11

Steve Armstrong pg 6

Pg. 9

Pg. 15

Pete Mills
Knoxville, TN

Allen Wheeler

Cas Cox

Denny Shaffer

Don Rackard

Harold Long
1930-1998
Tennessee

Pg. 1

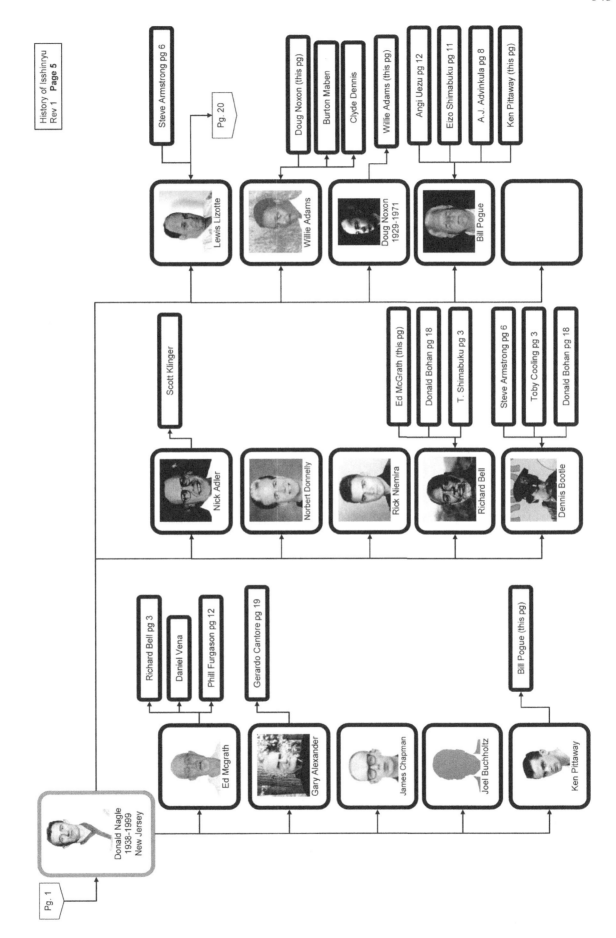

History of Isshinryu
Rev 1   **Page 5**

Steve Armstrong pg 6

Pg. 20

Doug Noxon (this pg)

Burton Maben

Clyde Dennis

Willie Adams (this pg)

Angi Uezu pg 12

Eizo Shimabuku pg 11

A.J. Advinkula pg 8

Ken Pittaway (this pg)

Lewis Lizotte

Willie Adams

Doug Noxon 1929-1971

Bill Pogue

Scott Klinger

Ed McGrath (this pg)

Donald Bohan 18

T. Shimabuku pg 3

Steve Armstrong pg 6

Toby Cooling pg 3

Donald Bohan 18

Nick Adler

Norbert Donnelly

Rick Niemira

Richard Bell

Dennis Bootle

Richard Bell pg 3

Daniel Vena

Phill Furgason pg 12

Gerardo Cantore pg 19

Bill Pogue (this pg)

Ed Mcgrath

Gary Alexander

James Chapman

Joel Buchholtz

Ken Pittaway

Donald Nagle 1938-1999 New Jersey

Pg. 1

144

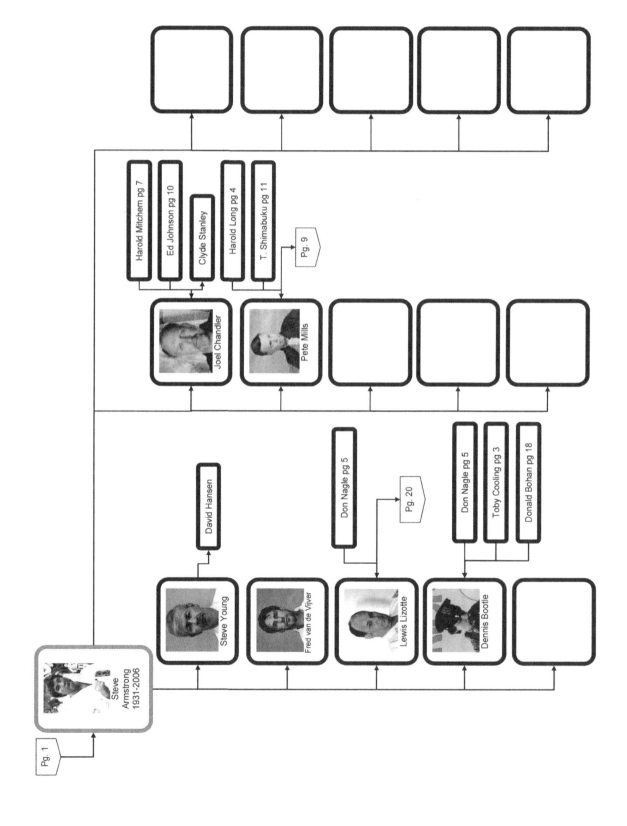

History of Isshinyu
Rev 1   **Page 6**

Steve Armstrong 1931-2006
Pg. 1

Steve Young — David Hansen
Fred van de Vijver
Lewis Lizotte — Don Nagle pg 5 / Pg. 20
Dennis Bootle — Don Nagle pg 5 / Toby Cooling pg 3 / Donald Bohan pg 18

Joel Chandler — Harold Mitchem pg 7 / Ed Johnson pg 10 / Clyde Stanley
Pete Mills — Harold Long pg 4 / T. Shimabuku pg 11 / Pg. 9

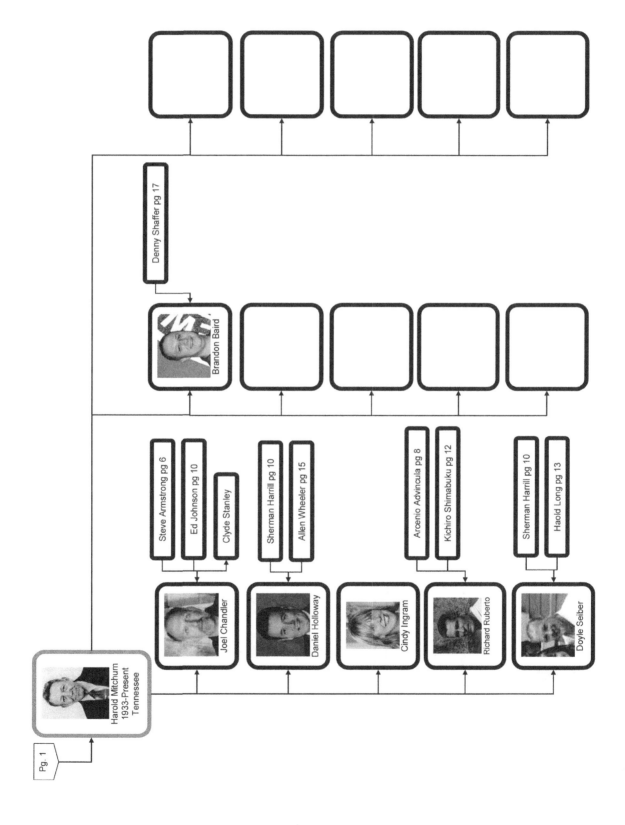

Pg. 1

146

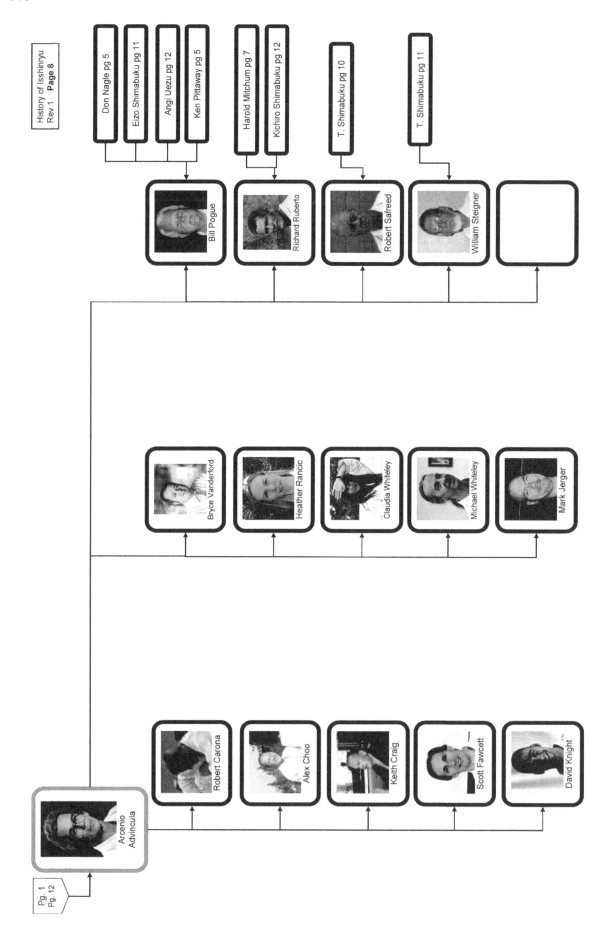

History of Isshinryu
Rev 1 Page 8

Don Nagle pg 5
Eizo Shimabuku pg 11
Angi Uezu pg 12
Ken Pittaway pg 5

Harold Mitchum pg 7
Kichiro Shimabuku pg 12

T. Shimabuku pg 10

T. Shimabuku pg 11

Bill Pogue
Richard Ruberto
Robert Safreed
William Steigner

Bryce Vanderford
Heather Rancic
Claudia Whiteley
Michael Whiteley
Mark Jerger

Arcenio Advincula

Robert Carona
Alex Choo
Keith Craig
Scott Fawcett
David Knight

Pg. 1
Pg. 12

History of Isshinryu
Rev 1 **Page 8**

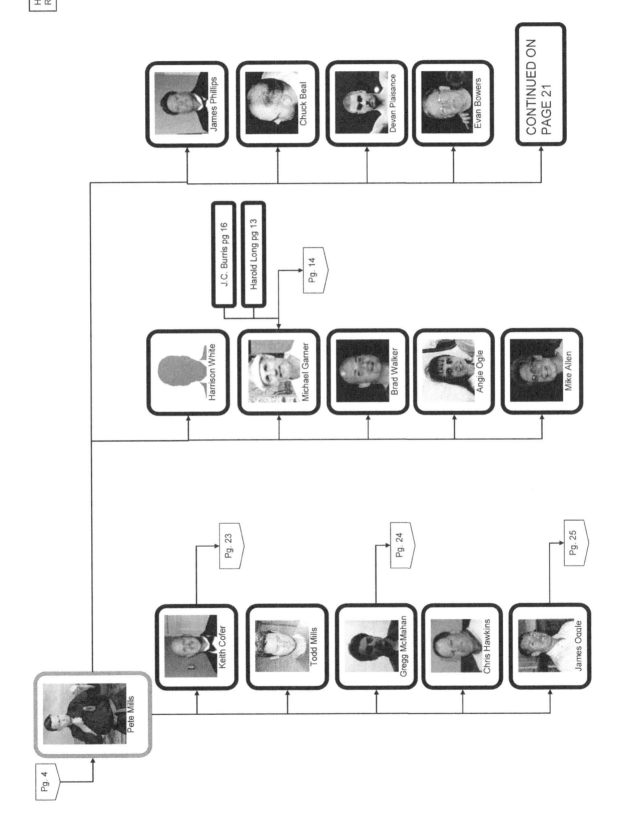

James Phillips

Chuck Beal

Devan Plaisance

Evan Bowers

CONTINUED ON PAGE 21

J.C. Burris pg 16

Harold Long pg 13

Pg. 14

Harrison White

Michael Garner

Brad Walker

Angie Ogle

Mike Allen

Pg. 23

Pg. 24

Pg. 25

Keith Cofer

Todd Mills

Gregg McMahan

Chris Hawkins

James Oggle

Pete Mills

Pg. 4

148

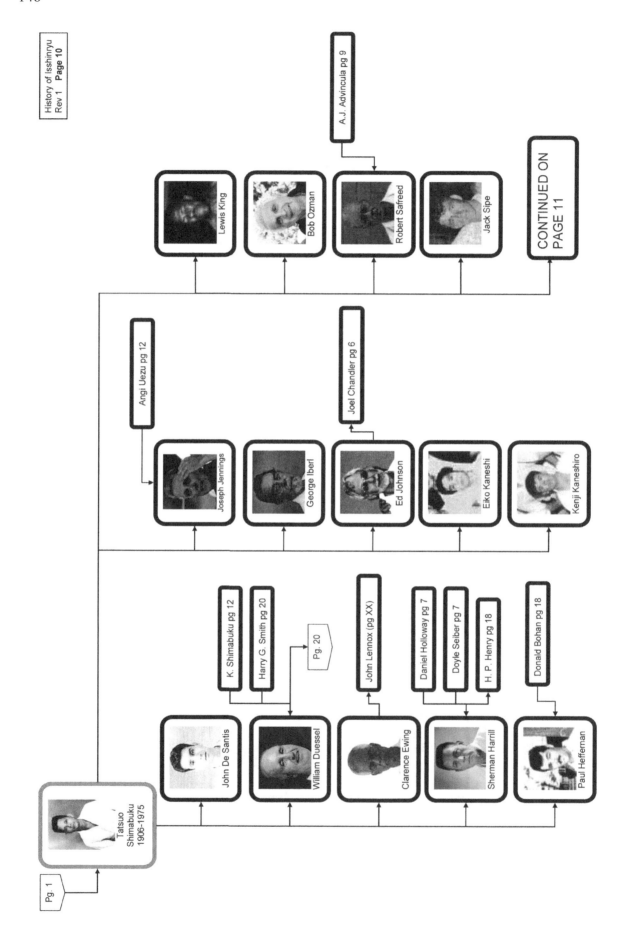

CONTINUED ON PAGE 11

A.J. Advincula pg 9

Lewis King

Bob Ozman

Robert Safreed

Jack Sipe

Angi Uezu pg 12

Joel Chandler pg 6

Joseph Jennings

George Iberl

Ed Johnson

Eiko Kaneshi

Kenji Kaneshiro

K. Shimabuku pg 12

Harry G. Smith pg 20

Pg. 20

John Lennox (pg XX)

Daniel Holloway pg 7

Doyle Seiber pg 7

H. P. Henry pg 18

Donald Bohan pg 18

John De Santis

William Duessel

Clarence Ewing

Sherman Harrill

Paul Heffernan

Tatsuo Shimabuku 1906-1975

Pg. 1

Tatsuo Shimabuku 1906-1975

Pg. 1

Shinsho Ciso Shimabuku — A.J. Advincula pg 8

Eizo Shimabuku — Bill Pogue pg 5

Art Smiley — Harry Smith pg 20

Harry G Smith — Pg. 20

Joe Smith — Harold Long pg 13 / Alan Wheeler pg 15 / Dan Jones pg 15

Duncan Squire

Al Squire

William Steigner — A.J. Advincula pg 8

Kensho Tokumura

Walt Van Gilson

Frank Van Lenten

David Zaslow

Tom Lewis — Reese Rigby / Rudy Rigby

Jack Eckenrode — Ed Brown

Pete Mills — Harold Long pg 4 / Steve Armstrong pg 6 / Pg. 9

150

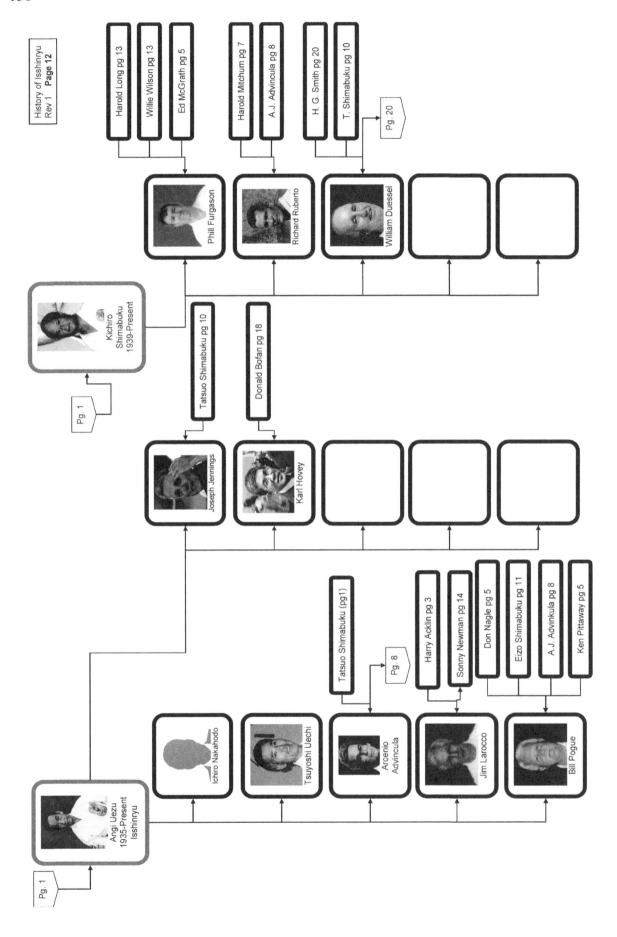

Harold Long pg 13
Willie Wilson pg 13
Ed McGrath pg 5
Harold Mitchum pg 7
A.J. Advincula pg 8
H. G. Smith pg 20
T. Shimabuku pg 10

Pg. 20

Phill Furgason
Richard Ruberto
William Duessel

Kichiro Shimabuku 1939-Present

Pg. 1

Tatsuo Shimabuku pg 10
Donald Bofan pg 18

Joseph Jennings
Karl Hovey

Tatsuo Shimabuku (pg1)

Pg. 8

Harry Acklin pg 3
Sonny Newman pg 14
Don Nagle pg 5
Eizo Shimabuku pg 11
A.J. Advinkula pg 8
Ken Pittaway pg 5

Ichiro Nakahodo
Tsuyoshi Uechi
Arcenio Advincula
Jim Larocco
Bill Pogue

Angi Uezu 1935-Present Isshinryu

Pg. 1

151

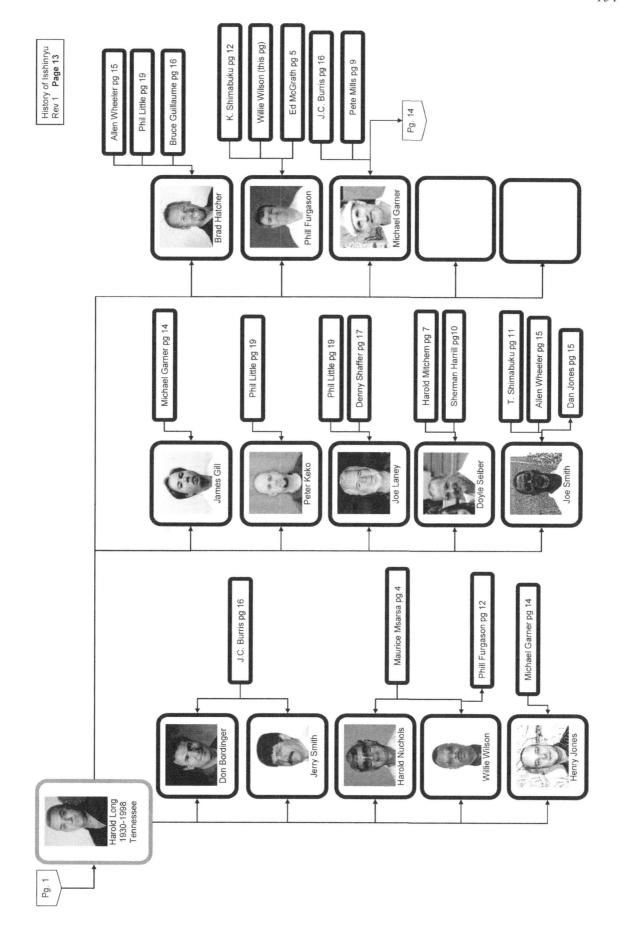

152

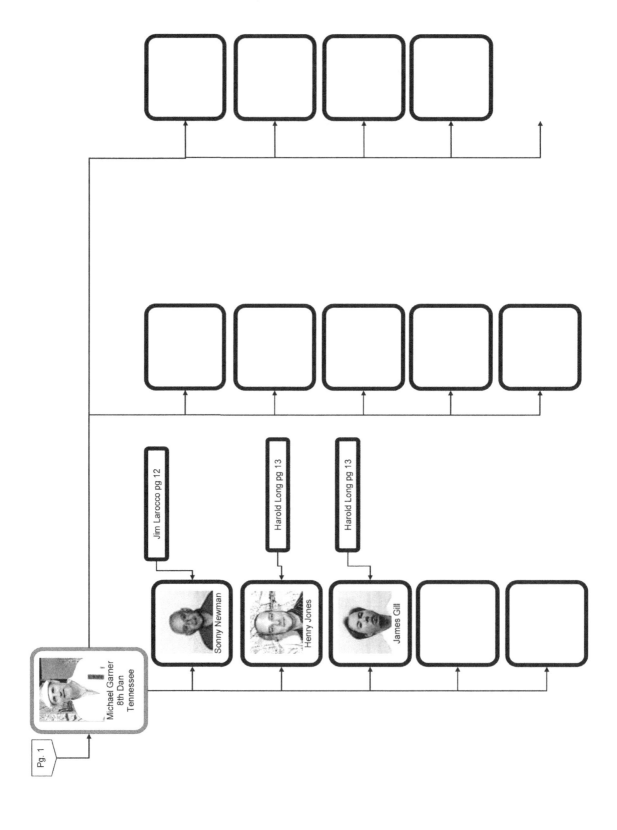

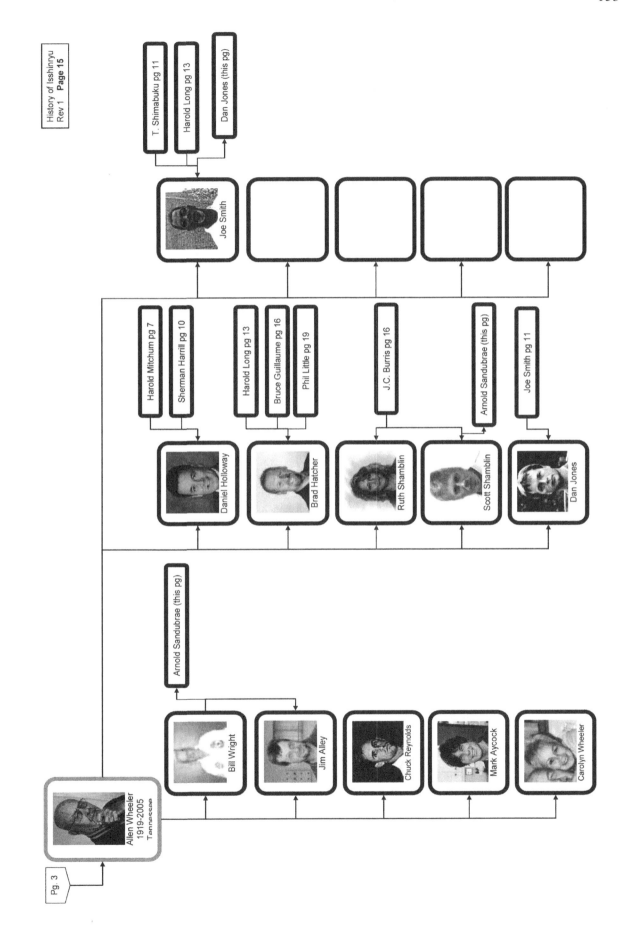

History of Isshinryu
Rev 1 **Page 15**

T. Shimabuku pg 11

Harold Long pg 13

Dan Jones (this pg)

Joe Smith

Harold Mitchum pg 7

Sherman Harrill pg 10

Harold Long pg 13

Bruce Guillaume pg 16

Phil Little pg 19

J.C. Burris pg 16

Arnold Sandubrae (this pg)

Joe Smith pg 11

Daniel Holloway

Brad Hatcher

Ruth Shamblin

Scott Shamblin

Dan Jones

Arnold Sandubrae (this pg)

Bill Wright

Jim Alley

Chuck Reynolds

Mark Aycock

Carolyn Wheeler

Allen Wheeler
1919-2005
Tennessee

Pg. 3

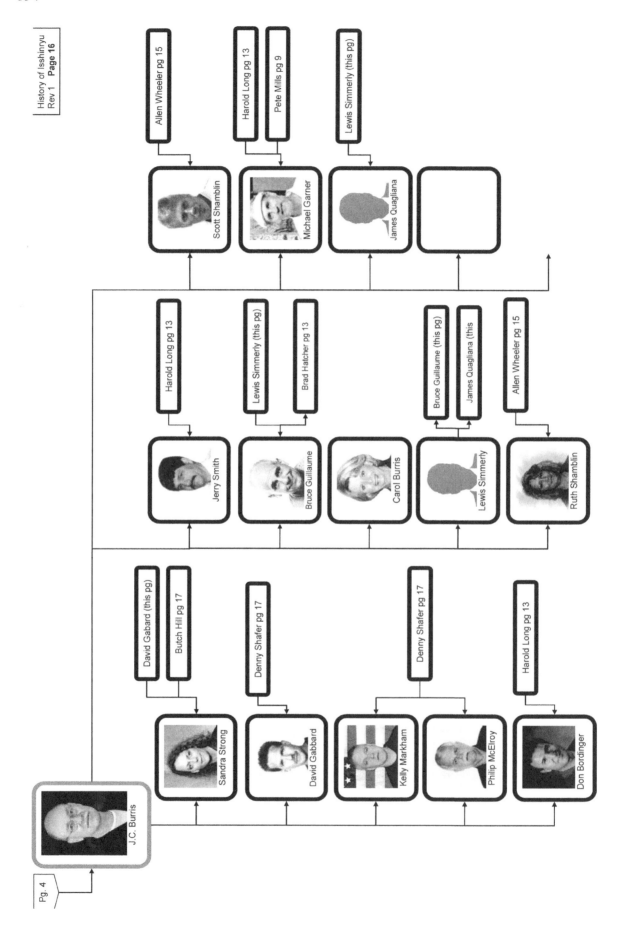

Allen Wheeler pg 15

Harold Long pg 13

Pete Mills pg 9

Lewis Simmerly (this pg)

Scott Shamblin

Michael Garner

James Quagliana

Harold Long 13

Lewis Simmerly (this pg)

Brad Hatcher pg 13

Bruce Guillaume (this pg)

James Quagliana (this

Allen Wheeler pg 15

Jerry Smith

Bruce Guillaume

Carol Burris

Lewis Simmerly

Ruth Shamblin

David Gabard (this pg)

Butch Hill pg 17

Denny Shafer pg 17

Denny Shafer pg 17

Harold Long pg 13

Sandra Strong

David Gabbard

Kelly Markham

Philip McElroy

Don Bordinger

J.C. Burris

Pg. 4

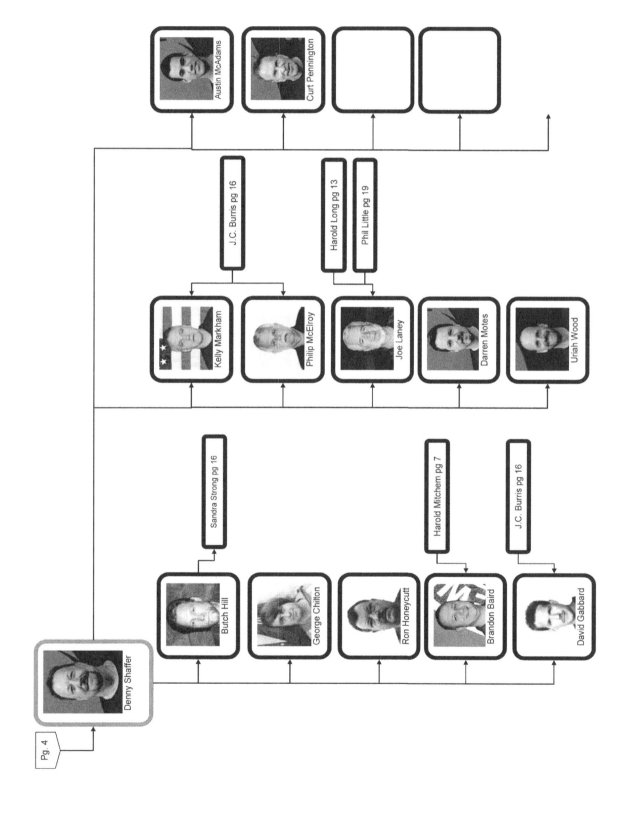

Austin McAdams

Curt Pennington

J.C. Burris pg 16

Harold Long pg 13

Phil Little pg 19

Kelly Markham

Philip McElroy

Joe Laney

Darren Motes

Uriah Wood

Sandra Strong pg 16

Harold Mitchem pg 7

J.C. Burris pg 16

Butch Hill

George Chilton

Ron Honeycutt

Brandon Baird

David Gabbard

Denny Shaffer

Pg. 4

156

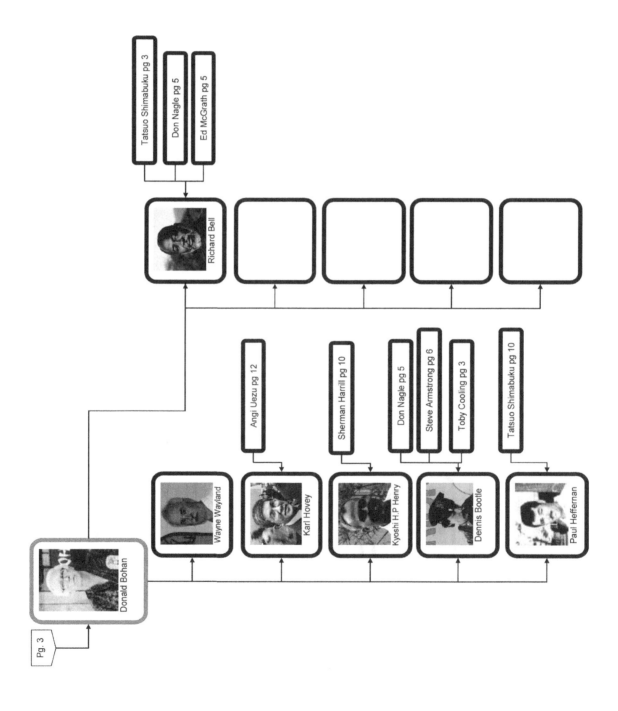

157

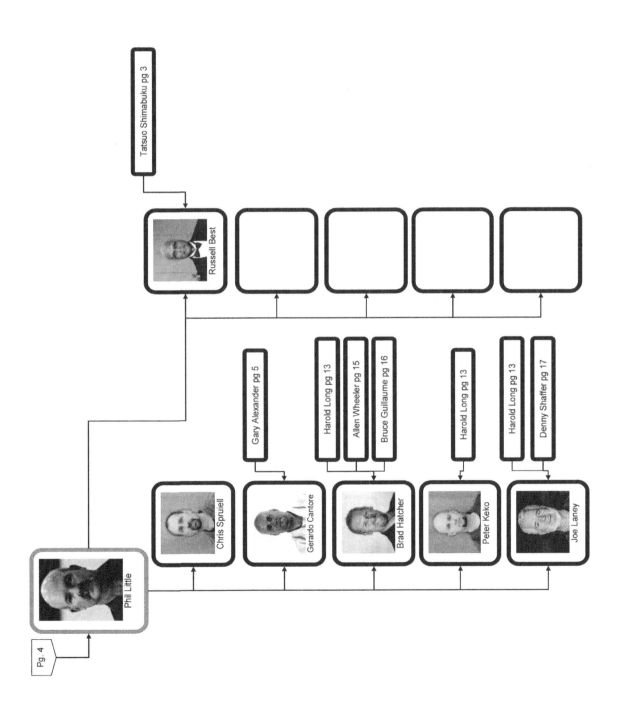

158

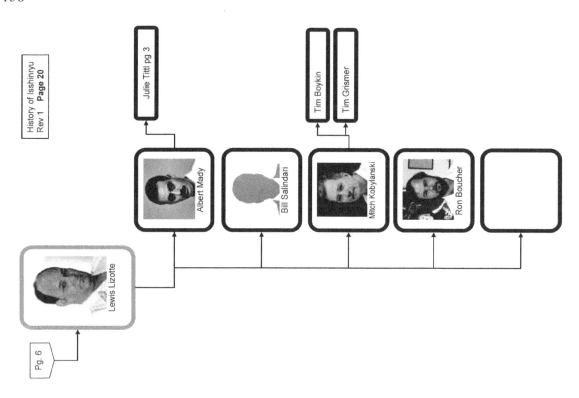

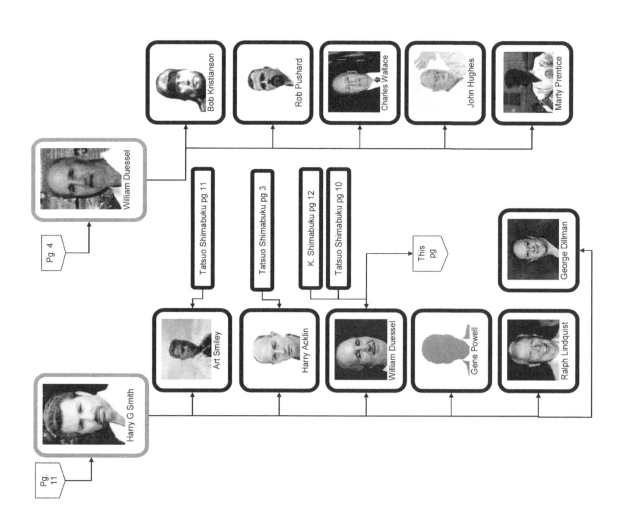

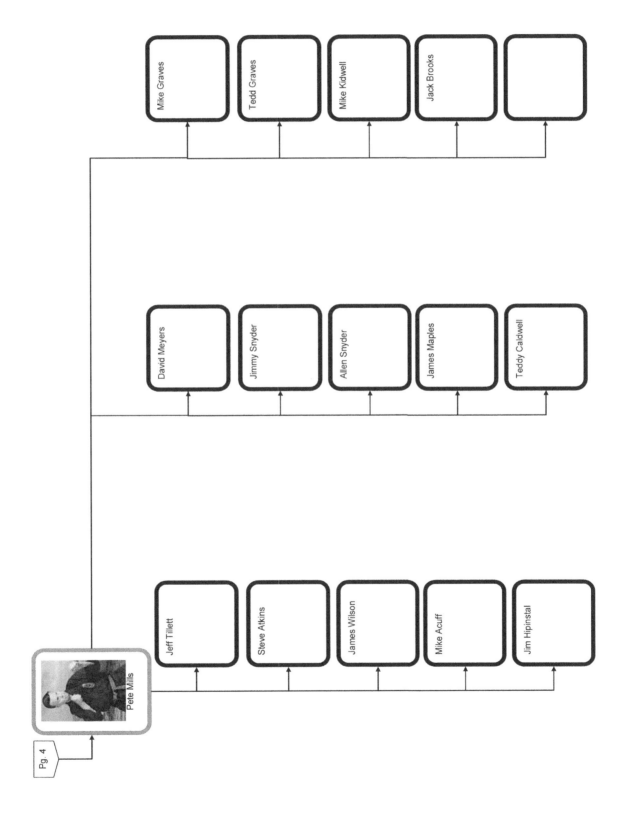

Mike Graves

Tedd Graves

Mike Kidwell

Jack Brooks

David Meyers

Jimmy Snyder

Allen Snyder

James Maples

Teddy Caldwell

Jeff Tillett

Steve Atkins

James Wilson

Mike Acuff

Jim Hipinstal

Pete Mills

Pg. 4

160

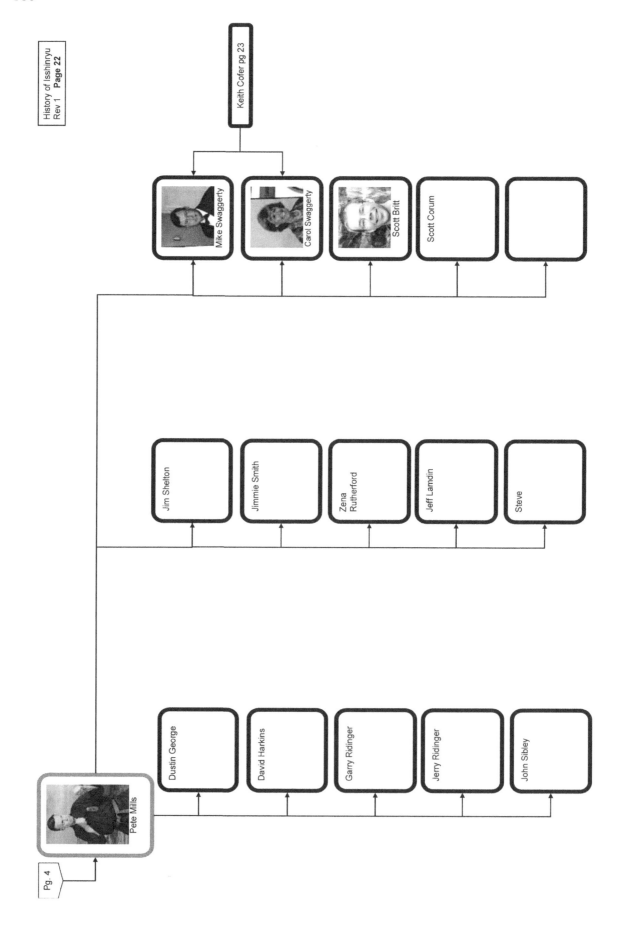

161

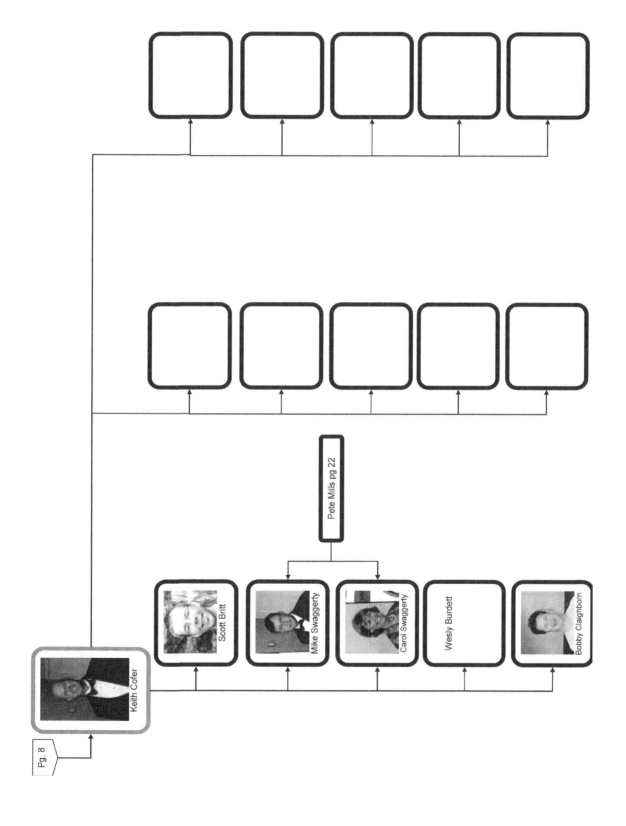

Keith Cofer

Pg. 8

Pete Mills pg 22

Scott Britt

Mike Swaggerty

Carol Swaggerty

Wesly Burdett

Bobby Claighborn

162

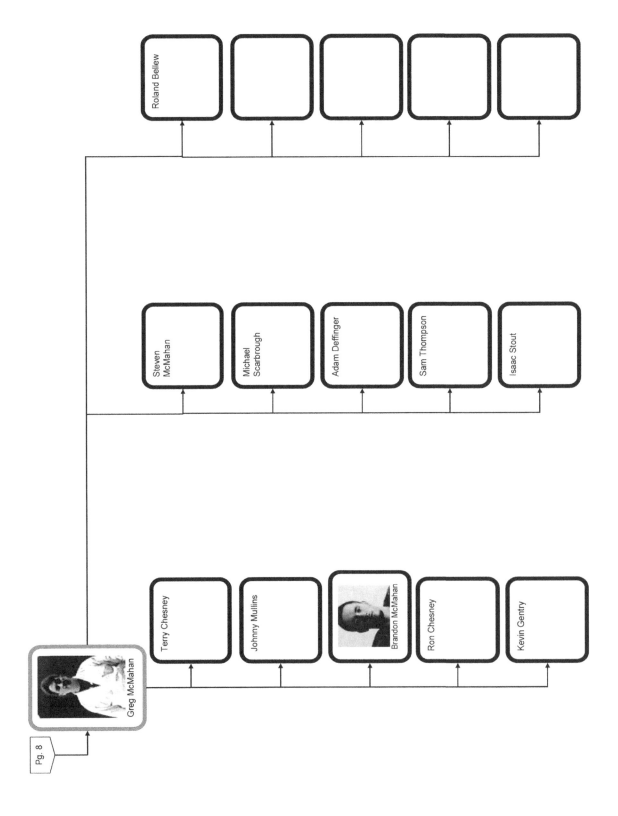

Roland Bellew

Steven McMahan

Michael Scarbrough

Adam Deffinger

Sam Thompson

Isaac Stout

Terry Chesney

Johnny Mullins

Brandon McMahan

Ron Chesney

Kevin Gentry

Greg McMahan

Pg. 8

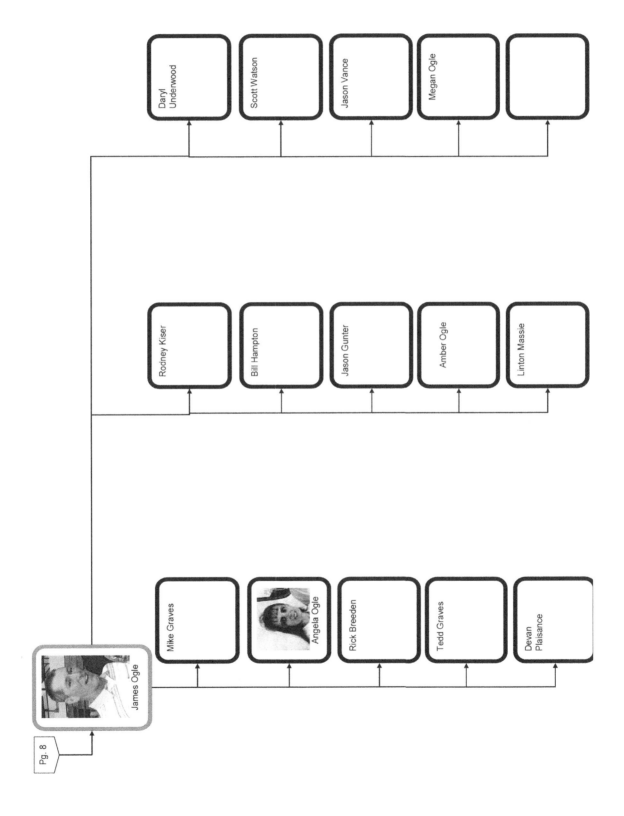

Daryl Underwood

Scott Watson

Jason Vance

Megan Ogle

Rodney Kiser

Bill Hampton

Jason Gunter

Amber Ogle

Linton Massie

Mike Graves

Angela Ogle

Rick Breeden

Tedd Graves

Devan Plaisance

James Ogle

Pg. 8

164

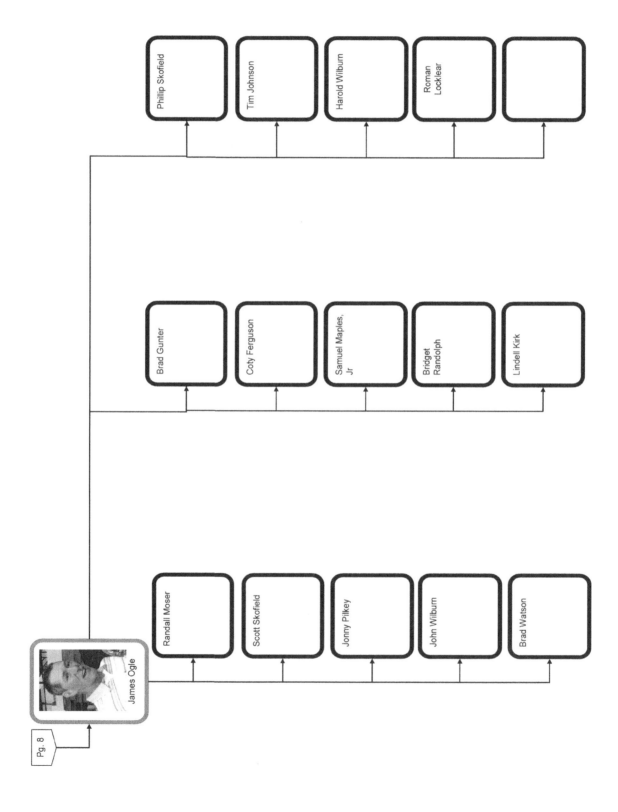

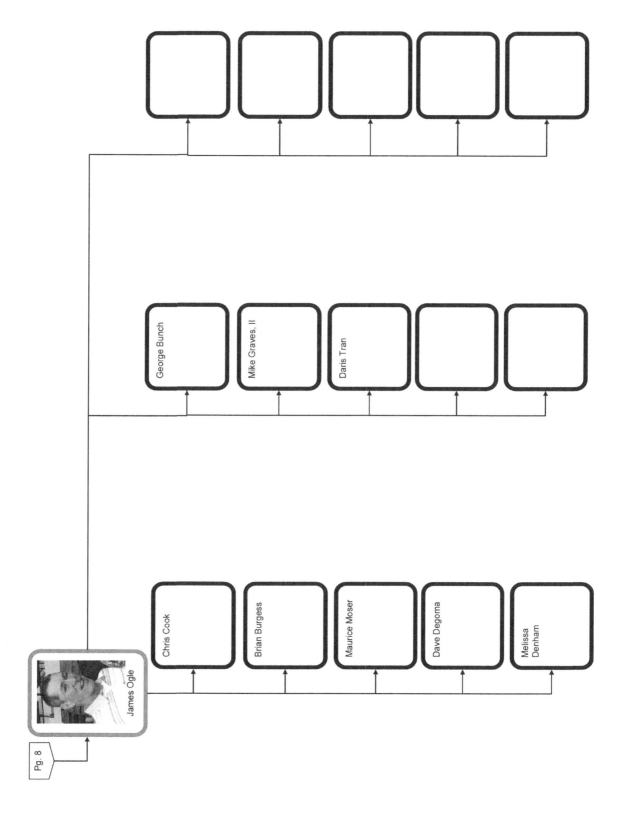

165

MARTIAL ARTS TOPIC SUMMARIES

Basic Guidelines for Sparring

1. **Keep your hands up!** You may see black belts lowering their hands – we can do that because we can judge distance and reaction time. Under belts need to keep both hands up at all times.

2. **Never back up more than two steps.** This gives your opponent a sense of power, and puts you in a mindset of retreat. Also, in a real fight, you may not know what is behind you. Instead, circle around or dodge on a 45 degree angle.

3. **Keep your eyes open.** This is going to take some practice. An old saying is, "You are knocked out by the one you did not see".

4. **Do not duck.** Bending over to avoid a punch invites a knee or kick into the face. Either block, back up, or squat slightly.

5. **No blind techniques.** Spinning around with a back fist without looking first is a bad idea! Either he will have backed up, then come back in with a counter attack, or he will have closed the distance because he saw you turn your back and you will elbow him in the face (I know–I have been on the receiving end of that!)

6. **Watch your opponents' sternum.** Experienced fighters will try to mislead you if you watch their eyes. Watching the sternum will allow you to see the torso move in preparation for a punch.

7. **Agree on a level of contact.** Under belts will always be no contact or light contact. Upper belts have the choice to go farther, but all ranks should agree with their partner before sparring. If your partner is using more contact than you are comfortable with, ask him to take it down or ask to spar someone else.

8. **Control your temper.** We are here to learn. If I see someone getting mad, I will stop the match. If someone leaves a match without bowing out, they are not welcome at this dojo.

9. **Watch your targets.** Attacks to the throat, eyes, spine, knees, temple, and back of head are not allowed. While good on the street, they are far too dangerous to practice in free sparring.

10. **Always have a cup and mouthpiece.** This is just common sense! The night you do not have them is the night you will wish you did!

Grappling 101

Remember, the instant you feel pain, tap!
If you feel someone tap, release immediately!
DO NOT go all out – experiment, work for position, and apply techniques carefully. Try to learn, not to win!

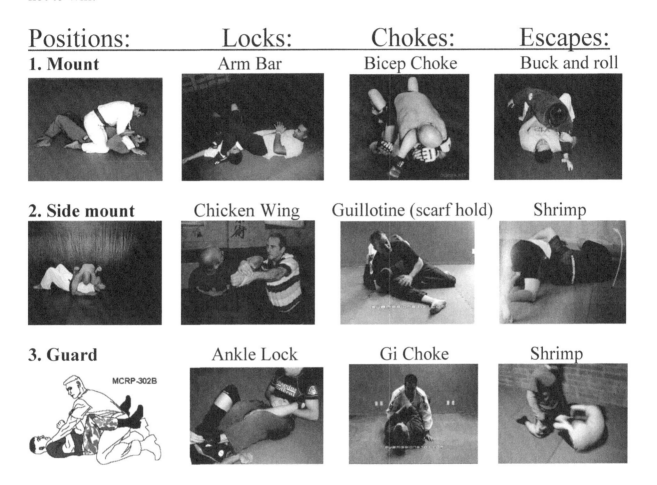

Positions:	Locks:	Chokes:	Escapes:
1. Mount	Arm Bar	Bicep Choke	Buck and roll
2. Side mount	Chicken Wing	Guillotine (scarf hold)	Shrimp
3. Guard	Ankle Lock	Gi Choke	Shrimp

Getting up safely from the ground

1. Hands up to protect face
2. Post up on opposite arm/leg
3. Kick opponent in knee
4. Bring foot back to hand
5. Stand up

Competing in Tournaments

Kata

- Always start and end on the same spot.
- Look before changing direction.
- <u>Kei Very Loudly!</u> This separates you from the other competitors.
- Make every move distinct – put a slight pause between movements so the judges can identify every move.
- Never make "face fouls." (grimacing when you make a mistake)
- You will be judged on:
  - Power
  - Speed
  - Precision
  - Balance
  - Focus
  - Accuracy
- When in doubt, bow.
- Speak loudly to the judges, looking at each in turn and ending with the center judge.
- Judges are looking for someone to run a kata as if they are actually in a fight- convince them that you are- through your expression, power, and determination.
- You are being judged before you ever step into the ring- be sharp, courteous, and a good sportsman at the ringside.
- Personal preference – do not watch those going before you, so you do not get discouraged.
- If you make a mistake, keep going. Judges will deduct a lot more points for having to restart your kata than for a mistake smoothly corrected. Different schools have variations to their katas – they may not even realize it was a mistake!

Competing in Tournaments

Sparring

- Keep your eyes up when bowing.
- If you injure your opponent, turn and kneel until the center judge calls you.
- Even if you make contact with your opponent, <u>keep sparing</u> until the center judge calls a point.
- 3 main styles of fighting:
    1. Aggressive – attacking the instant the judge says go.
    2. Passive – waiting, feeling out your opponent and then counter-striking.
    3. Retreating – running around the ring, waiting for the opponent to overextend trying to reach you.

    Know what you are best at, and how to defend against all 3.
- Claim the center of the ring and make your opponent move around you.
- If your points are not being called, maneuver around so the judges can see.
- Be careful to watch the opponents sparring before you, so you know what to expect.
- Never get forced outside of the ring- circle around or move on a 45° angle.
- Always have a light warm-up before competition.
- Remember – the judges are human. You may lose some tournaments that you should have won. Just remember, this is just a game, and other times the overlooked points will work in your favor.

Example Training Sessions

Below are some methods to train at home to increase your skills, while using enough variety to keep it interesting. It is HIGHLY encouraged to pair your karate training with a regular exercise program and regulated diet.

1. Video yourself running a kata, play back and critique
2. Targeting a towel hung over the shower curtain rod - try to hit at full speed with control, so towel does not move back
3. Run kata focusing on single attribute: stance, hands in position, looking before you turn, kiais, balance, speed, precision, bunkai, breathing, etc.
4. Working on a heavy bag (or a pillow propped up) for power
5. Snuff out a candle with the air from a punch or kick (speed/control training)
6. Shadow box
7. Watch YouTube of Tatsuo, other style running the same kata, bunkai, etc.
8. Read Martial Arts related book
9. Pull difficult moves from kata and run like charts, 10 times each side to iron them out
10. Run personalized katas 1-4
11. Practice break falls
12. Change up how you run kata - face a different direction, wear shoes and a coat, blindfolded (and see where you end up!), in a pool, holding weights, backwards, in your head, up a hill, in gravel, etc.
13. Run the upper body portion of a kata as you jog
14. Use wooden dummy (or equivalent) for speed / blocking drills

Sample training sessions

20 Min Bunkai session	
1	Warm up / stretch
4	2 katas slow for application
2	1 kata on Wooden Dummy (bag)
4	3 katas full speed/power
3	Watch 1 Tatsuo kata
3	Run 3 moves from kata like charts
2	Run a personalized kata 5 times
1	Easy Sanchin cool down

20 Min Speed/Power session	
1	Warm up / stretch
3	2 katas with snap
6	towel/candle drills
1	Shadow box
3	2 katas with weights (slow!)
2	Heavy bag
3	2 katas full power
1	Easy Sanchin cool down

40 Min General training session	
2	Warm up / stretch
1	Run stance kata 2 times
10	Charts 3 times each side
4	3 katas slowly for form
3	Watch 1 Tatsuo video
6	Run 1 kata 4 times, focusing on a different attribute each time
4	Run 3 kata full speed / power
5	Run all 3 personalized katas twice
2	Break falls / getting up safe
2	Heavy bag or wooden dummy
1	Easy Sanchin cool down

10 Min Better than nothing session	
4	3 kata normal speed
2	Run a personalized kata 3 times
3	2 kata full power
1	Heavy bag

TN Laws on Self-Defense

Retrieved from www.TN.gov on March 30, 2017
TENNESSEE CODE ANNOTATED

39-11-611. Self-defense.

(a) As used in this section, unless the context otherwise requires:

(1) "Business" means a commercial enterprise or establishment owned by a person as all or part of the person's livelihood or is under the owner's control or who is an employee or agent of the owner with responsibility for protecting persons and property and shall include the interior and exterior premises of the business;

(2) [Deleted by 2016 amendment.]

(3) "Curtilage" means the area surrounding a dwelling that is necessary, convenient and habitually used for family purposes and for those activities associated with the sanctity of a person's home;

(4) "Deadly force" means the use of force intended or likely to cause death or serious bodily injury;

(5) "Dwelling" means a building or conveyance of any kind, including any attached porch, whether the building or conveyance is temporary or permanent, mobile or immobile, that has a roof over it, including a tent, and is designed for or capable of use by people;

(6) "Nuclear power reactor facility" means a reactor designed to produce heat for electric generation, for producing radiation or fissionable materials, or for reactor component testing, and does not include a reactor used for research purposes;

(7) "Nuclear security officer" means a person who meets the requirements of 10 CFR Part 73, Appendix B, who is an employee or an employee of a contractor of the owner of a nuclear power reactor facility, and who has been appointed or designated by the owner of a nuclear power reactor facility to provide security for the facility;

(8) "Residence" means a dwelling in which a person resides, either temporarily or permanently, or is visiting as an invited guest, or any dwelling, building or other appurtenance within the curtilage of the residence; and

(9) "Vehicle" means any motorized vehicle that is self-propelled and designed for use on public highways to transport people or property.

(b) (1) Notwithstanding § 39-17-1322, a person who is not engaged in unlawful activity and is in a place where the person has a right to be has no duty to retreat before threatening or using force against another person when and to the degree the person reasonably believes the force is immediately necessary to protect against the other's use or attempted use of unlawful force.

(2) Notwithstanding § 39-17-1322, a person who is not engaged in unlawful activity and is in a place where the person has a right to be has no duty to retreat before threatening or using force intended or likely to cause death or serious bodily injury, if:

    (A) The person has a reasonable belief that there is an imminent danger of death or serious bodily injury;

    (B) The danger creating the belief of imminent death or serious bodily injury is real, or honestly believed to be real at the time; and

    (C) The belief of danger is founded upon reasonable grounds.

(c) Any person using force intended or likely to cause death or serious bodily injury within a residence, business, dwelling or vehicle is presumed to have held a reasonable belief of imminent death or serious bodily injury to self, family, a member of the household or a person visiting as an invited guest, when that force is used against another person, who unlawfully and forcibly enters or has unlawfully and forcibly entered the residence, business, dwelling or vehicle, and the person using defensive force knew or had reason to believe that an unlawful and forcible entry occurred.

(d) The presumption established in subsection (c) shall not apply, if:

    (1) The person against whom the force is used has the right to be in or is a lawful resident of the dwelling, business, residence, or vehicle, such as an owner, lessee, or titleholder; provided, that the person is not prohibited from entering the dwelling, business, residence, or occupied vehicle by an order of protection, injunction for protection from domestic abuse, or a court order of no contact against that person;

    (2) The person against whom the force is used is attempting to remove a person or persons who is a child or grandchild of, or is otherwise in the lawful custody or under the lawful guardianship of, the person against whom the defensive force is used;

    (3) Notwithstanding § 39-17-1322, the person using force is engaged in an unlawful activity or is using the dwelling, business, residence, or occupied vehicle to further an unlawful activity; or

    (4) The person against whom force is used is a law enforcement officer, as defined in § 39-11-106, who enters or attempts to enter a dwelling, business, residence, or vehicle in the performance of the officer's official duties, and the officer identified the officer in accordance with any applicable law, or the person using force knew or reasonably should have known that the person entering or attempting to enter was a law enforcement officer.

(e) The threat or use of force against another is not justified:

(1) If the person using force consented to the exact force used or attempted by the other individual;

(2) If the person using force provoked the other individual's use or attempted use of unlawful force, unless:

(A) The person using force abandons the encounter or clearly communicates to the other the intent to do so; and

(B) The other person nevertheless continues or attempts to use unlawful force against the person; or

(3) To resist a halt at a roadblock, arrest, search, or stop and frisk that the person using force knows is being made by a law enforcement officer, unless:

(A) The law enforcement officer uses or attempts to use greater force than necessary to make the arrest, search, stop and frisk, or halt; and

(B) The person using force reasonably believes that the force is immediately necessary to protect against the law enforcement officer's use or attempted use of greater force than necessary.

(f) A nuclear security officer is authorized to use deadly force under the following circumstances:

(1) Deadly force appears reasonably necessary to prevent or impede an act, or attempted act, of radiological sabotage at a nuclear power reactor facility, including, but not limited to, situations where a person is attempting to, or has, unlawfully or forcefully entered a nuclear power reactor facility, and where adversary tactics are employed to attempt an act of radiological sabotage, such as, but not limited to:

(A) Use of firearms or small arms;

(B) Use of explosive devices;

(C) Use of incendiary devices;

(D) Use of vehicle borne improvised explosive devices;

(E) Use of water borne improvised explosive devices;

(F) Breaching of barriers; and

(G) Use of other adversary or terrorist tactics which could be employed to attempt an act of radiological sabotage;

(2) Deadly force appears reasonably necessary to protect the nuclear security officer or another person if the nuclear security officer reasonably believes there is an imminent danger of death or serious bodily injury;

(3) Deadly force appears reasonably necessary to prevent the imminent infliction or threatened infliction of death or serious bodily harm or the sabotage of an occupied facility by explosives;

(4) Deadly force appears reasonably necessary to prevent the theft, sabotage, or unauthorized control of special nuclear material from a nuclear power reactor facility; or

(5) Deadly force reasonably appears to be necessary to apprehend or prevent the escape of a person reasonably believed to:
    (A) Have committed an offense of the nature specified under this subsection (f); or
    (B) Be escaping by use of a weapon or explosive or who otherwise poses an imminent danger of death or serious bodily harm to nuclear security officers or others unless apprehended without delay.

39-11-612. Defense of third person.
A person is justified in threatening or using force against another to protect a third person, if:
    (1) Under the circumstances as the person reasonably believes them to be, the person would be justified under § 39-11-611 in threatening or using force to protect against the use or attempted use of unlawful force reasonably believed to be threatening the third person sought to be protected; and
    (2) The person reasonably believes that the intervention is immediately necessary to protect the third person.

39-11-613. Protection of life or health.

A person is justified in threatening or using force, but not deadly force, against another, when and to the degree the person reasonably believes the force is immediately necessary to prevent the other from committing suicide or from the self-infliction of serious bodily injury.

39-11-614. Protection of property.

(a) A person in lawful possession of real or personal property is justified in threatening or using force against another, when and to the degree it is reasonably believed the force is immediately necessary to prevent or terminate the other's trespass on the land or unlawful interference with the property.

(b) A person who has been unlawfully dispossessed of real or personal property is justified in threatening or using force against the other, when and to the degree it is reasonably believed the force is immediately necessary to reenter the land or recover the property, if the person threatens or uses the force immediately or in fresh pursuit after the dispossession:

(1) The person reasonably believes the other had no claim of right when the other dispossessed the person; and

(2) The other accomplished the dispossession by threatening or using force against the person.

(c) Unless a person is justified in using deadly force as otherwise provided by law, a person is not justified in using deadly force to prevent or terminate the other's trespass on real estate or unlawful interference with personal property.

39-11-615. Protection of third person's property.

A person is justified in threatening or using force against another to protect real or personal property of a third person, if, under the circumstances as the person reasonably believes them to be, the person would be justified under § 39-11-614 in threatening or using force to protect the person's own real or personal property.

39-11-616. Use of device to protect property.

(a) The justification afforded by §§ 39-11-614 and 39-11-615 extends to the use of a device for the purpose of protecting property, only if:

(1) The device is not designed to cause or known to create a substantial risk of causing death or serious bodily harm;

(2) The use of the particular device to protect the property from entry or trespass is reasonable under the circumstances as the person believes them to be; and

(3) The device is one customarily used for such a purpose, or reasonable care is taken to make known to probable intruders the fact that it is used.

(b) Nothing in this section shall affect the law regarding the use of animals to protect property or persons.

39-11-621. Use of deadly force by private citizen.

A private citizen, in making an arrest authorized by law, may use force reasonably necessary to accomplish the arrest of an individual who flees or resists the arrest; provided, that a private citizen cannot use or threaten to use deadly force except to the extent authorized under self-defense or defense of third person statutes, §§ 39-11-611 and 39-11-612.

39-11-622. Justification for use of force -- Exceptions -- Immunity from civil liability.

(a) (1) A person who uses force as permitted in §§ 39-11-611 -- 39-11-614 or § 29-34-201, is justified in using such force and is immune from civil liability for the use of such force, unless:

(A) The person against whom force was used is a law enforcement officer, as defined in § 39-11-106 who:

(i) Was acting in the performance of the officer's official duties; and

(ii) Identified the officer in accordance with any applicable law; or

(iii) The person using force knew or reasonably should have known that the person was a law enforcement officer; or

(B) The force used by the person resulted in property damage to or the death or injury of an innocent bystander or other person against whom the force used was not justified.

(b) The court shall award reasonable attorney's fees, court costs, compensation for loss of income, and all expenses incurred by a person in defense of any civil action brought against the person based upon the person's use of force, if the court finds that the defendant was justified in using such force pursuant to §§ 39-11-611 -- 39-11-614 or § 29-34-201.

Karate Resources

Websites:

http://petemillskarate.com/
History / Student Creed / Charts / Our Dojo homepage :)

http://www.isshinryukarate.com/
Web page of Kichiro Shimabuku, Okinawan head over Isshinryu. Videos of kata by Michael Calandra

www.youtube.com
Videos of Tatsuo running all katas, also of Ungi Uezu demonstrating bunkai.

http://www.msisshinryu.com/masters/index2.shtml
A.J. Advincula's history of karate masters

http://www.traditionalokinawanmartialarts.com/isshinkaivideo/video.aspx
Videos of Advincula running all kata

http://www.theihof.com/
Hall of fame site, includes bios of all inductees (names you will hear throughout your martial arts career)

http://www.iika.org/
International Isshin~ryu Karate Association site. Tournament rules, black belt rank requirements, upcoming events (that are IIKA sanctioned)

http://www.ustmas.com/USTMAS/default.html
Tennessee Martial Arts University (Shihan Michael Garner). Upcoming events, history

http://www.iainabernethy.co.uk/
One of the world's formost practical karate masters - sign up for newsletter, has a podcast every month.

Books:

Isshinryu Chinto Kata: Secrets revealed
Javier Martinez
If you can get ANY in his series, it is well worth it - excellent breakdown of kata.

The Way of Kata
Lawrence Kane
Excellent book on Bunkai

An Introduction to applied karate
Ian Abernathy
Free e-book from http://www.iainabernethy.com/Applied_Karate.pdf

The application of the Pinan / Heian katas
Ian Abernathy
Free e-book from http://www.iainabernethy.com/Pinan_Heian_Series.pdf

The Encyclopedia of Dim-Mak
Erle Montaigue
Good overview of pressure points, if you discount all the bunk and bologna.

Karate Breaking Techniques
Jack Hibbard
The best book on how to break.

Dynamics of Isshinryu Karate (3 book set)
Out of print, but a very good resource to have if you can get it.

Art of War
Sun Tzu
The classical treaties on war tactics and strategies, still used today by the military and business world.

Any book by Gichin Funakoshi, said by many to the founder of modern karate. Titles include:
Karate-do: my way of life
Karate-do Nyumon
The Twenty Precepts of Gichin Funakoshi
Karate-do Kyohan

Any book by Grandmaster Pete Mills, which can be purchased from him directly.

How to Practice Kata

Below is a summary of the scientific paper "Kata Practice as it Relates to Practical Application in Conflict" by Scott Britt, which was accepted to the Volume 8.1 edition of The Journal of Combat Sports and Martial Arts. The full article can be found at www.combatsports.edu.pl

Summary

Kata has the ability to get in more training that is still effective (possibly more effective) than could be gained with partner training alone as a result of added repetitions for muscle memory, combined with the possibility for full-power practice of dangerous strikes.

However, to have all of the benefits listed above, there are certain criteria that the training must meet or else the kata is impotent:

1. The practitioner must have a sound knowledge of the applications of the kata (without Bunkai, kata is meaningless)

2. The attackers MUST be vividly visualized during practice

3. The practitioner should stop if focus is lost and practice in short sessions

4. Physical practice must accompany mental practice

5. The kata should be performed sharply to prevent ingraining bad habits (repetition does not differentiate; it will ingrain the good and the bad, whatever is done repeatedly)

If all of these criteria are met, kata provides a powerful tool for the karate practitioner's tool box. Without kata practice, a student limits his or her growth and learning rate potential. For those who wish to excel at a faster rate than class time will allow, kata is a proven method of advancing skill though practice outside the dojo.

PERSONAL NOTES

184

Tournament Log

Date:_____

Name:_____

Tournament Name:_____

Tournament Location:_____

Divisions Entered:_____

Trophies/Medals Won:_____

Results/Comments:_____

_____

_____

_____

Date:_____

Name:_____

Tournament Name:_____

Tournament Location:_____

Divisions Entered:_____

Trophies/Medals Won:_____

Results/Comments:_____

_____

_____

_____

Tournament Log

Date:_____

Name:_____

Tournament Name:_____

Tournament Location:_____

Divisions Entered:_____

Trophies/Medals Won:_____

Results/Comments:_____

_____

_____

_____

Date:_____

Name:_____

Tournament Name:_____

Tournament Location:_____

Divisions Entered:_____

Trophies/Medals Won:_____

Results/Comments:_____

_____

_____

_____

Tournament Log

Date:_____

Name:_____

Tournament Name:_____

Tournament Location:_____

Divisions Entered:_____

Trophies/Medals Won:_____

Results/Comments:_____

_____

_____

_____

Date:_____

Name:_____

Tournament Name:_____

Tournament Location:_____

Divisions Entered:_____

Trophies/Medals Won:_____

Results/Comments:_____

_____

_____

_____

Tournament Log

Date:_____

Name:_____

Tournament Name:_____

Tournament Location:_____

Divisions Entered:_____

Trophies/Medals Won:_____

Results/Comments:_____

_____

_____

_____

Date:_____

Name:_____

Tournament Name:_____

Tournament Location:_____

Divisions Entered:_____

Trophies/Medals Won:_____

Results/Comments:_____

_____

_____

_____

Rank record

Use this section to document rank advancements, as well as any critique you received or things to correct by next belt.

Example:

Rank: _Yellow___ Date: _11/23/13_ Tested by: _Greg____

Notes: ___*Need to keep fingers together when I gouge, and make sure to look before I turn.*_____

Rank Record

Rank: _____ Date: _____ Tested by: _____

Notes: _____

_____

Rank: _____ Date: _____ Tested by: _____

Notes: _____

_____

Rank: _____ Date: _____ Tested by: _____

Notes: _____

_____

Rank: _____ Date: _____ Tested by: _____

Notes: _____

_____

Rank: _____ Date: _____ Tested by: _____

Notes: _____

_____

Rank: _____ Date: _____ Tested by: _____

Notes: _____

_____

Rank: _____ Date: _____ Tested by: _____

Notes: _____

Rank: _____ Date: _____ Tested by: _____

Notes: _____

Rank: _____ Date: _____ Tested by: _____

Notes: _____

Rank: _____ Date: _____ Tested by: _____

Notes: _____

Rank: _____ Date: _____ Tested by: _____

Notes: _____

Rank: _____ Date: _____ Tested by: _____

Notes: _____

Autographs

Use this section to get signatures from famous martial artists at seminars, visiting grandmasters, etc.

_____

Signature

_____ _____ _____

Print name   Date   Location

_____

Signature

_____ _____ _____

Print name   Date   Location

_____

Signature

_____ _____ _____

Print name   Date   Location

_____

Signature

_____ _____ _____

Print name   Date   Location

_____

Signature

_____ _____ _____

Print name   Date   Location

Appendix D – Signatures

_____

Signature

_____ _____ _____

Print name   Date   Location

Signature
_____

Print name _____ Date _____ Location _____

Signature
_____

Print name _____ Date _____ Location _____

Signature
_____

Print name _____ Date _____ Location _____

Signature
_____

Print name _____ Date _____ Location _____

Signature
_____

Print name _____ Date _____ Location _____

Signature
_____

Print name _____ Date _____ Location _____

Signature
_____

Print name _____ Date _____ Location _____

Notes

Made in the USA
Las Vegas, NV
07 July 2024

91984529R00109